Classical Economics

Reconsidered

THOMAS SOWELL

Classical Economics
Reconsidered

Princeton University Press

PRINCETON, NEW JERSEY

Copyright © 1974 by Princeton University Press
Published by Princeton University Press, Princeton, N.J.
In the U.K.: Princeton University Press, Guildford, Surrey
ALL RIGHTS RESERVED
Library of Congress Cataloging in Publication Data
will be found on the last printed page
of this book
Composed in Linotype Janson and
printed in the United States of America by
Princeton University Press
Princeton, New Jersey
ISBN 0-691-00358-0 (paperback edn.)
ISBN 0-691-04201-2 (hardcover edn.)
First Princeton Paperback printing, 1977

CONTENTS

A C K N O W L E D G M E N T S

I WISH to express my appreciation for comments on portions of this work by Professors William R. Allen and Earl A. Thompson of the University of California at Los Angeles and Professor Gerald P. O'Driscoll of the University of California at Santa Barbara.

Thomas Sowell

Classical Economics
Reconsidered

CHAPTER I

Social Philosophy

THE CLASSICAL PERIOD in the development of economics
is an important chapter in intellectual history, with general implications for the evolution of concepts, the dynamics of controversy, and basic problems of methodology. Yet too often the examples and insights it presents
are lost behind a veil of myths and stereotypes. Everyone
has heard of the classical economists' social conservatism,
blind faith in the market, denials of depression, and dis-
mal prognoses of subsistence wages. These have become
as axiomatic in the literature as they are grossly inac-
curate in fact.

Vague and shifting terms have become so common in
discussions of the classical economists that any recon-
sideration of them must begin with such basic questions
as who they were, what these particular individuals had
in common that causes them to share a common label, and
what their role was in the intellectual and social history
of their time. The main substantive propositions of classical economics still require enumeration, definition, and
analysis, despite—and to some extent, because of—the
voluminous interpretive literature which has accumulated
over the years. The criticisms of the classical economists,
by their contemporaries and by modern interpreters,
must also be considered in order to understand their role

and their relevance to modern economics and to intellectual history generally.

THE MEANING OF CLASSICAL ECONOMICS

Who was "classical"? Definitions range from that of Karl Marx, who coined the term, to that of John Maynard Keynes, who gave it its broadest meaning. For Marx, classical economics began with Sir William Petty and ended with Ricardo in England, and covered the period from Boisguillebert to Sismondi in France[1]—in both countries, spanning the period from the turn of the eighteenth century to the second decade of the nineteenth century. The distinguishing feature of classical economics, as seen by Marx, was its emphasis on human relationships in the economic process—"economic sociology" in modern terms—as contrasted with "vulgar economics," which emphasized economic phenomena narrowly defined.[2] The classical economists had, of course, also dealt with economic phenomena in the narrow, impersonal sense—as did Marx himself—but, according to Marx, only as part of an explanation of more general social relationships. Marx's criticism of the classical economists, in this regard, was that they did not clearly *separate* the two kinds of inquiries on different levels of abstraction[3] (as he did in the three volumes of *Capital.*[4]

[1] Karl Marx, *Critique of Political Economy* (Chicago: Charles H. Kerr & Co., 1904), p. 56.

[2] Karl Marx, *Capital* (Chicago: Charles H. Kerr & Co., 1906), I, 93n.

[3] Karl Marx, *Theories of Surplus Value* (New York: International Publishers, 1952), p. 202.

[4] See Thomas Sowell, "Marx's *Capital* After One Hundred Years," *Canadian Journal of Economics and Political Science*, February 1967, pp. 66–67.

Clearly Marx conceived of the classical economists as forerunners of Marxian economics, as suggested by the title of his mammoth history of economic thought: *Theories of Surplus Value.*

The Keynesian definition of classical economics was no less tendentious and egocentric. It included all of the post-Ricardian economists who had not repudiated Say's Law.[5] This led him to include among the "classical" works writings only a few years old at the time his *General Theory* appeared—writings whose doctrines appeared to a leading contemporary to be "quite as strange and novel as the doctrines of Mr. Keynes himself."[6] Moreover, there were serious questions raised from the outset as to whether *any* identifiable set of economists had ever believed the things attributed by Keynes to the "classical economists" as he defined them. Certainly no major economist from David Hume to the present has ever claimed (or suggested) that the velocity of circulation of money remains constant through all phases of the business cycle, which Keynes treated as a major classical doctrine to be refuted.[7] Indeed, most of the classical and neoclassical economists were quite explicit that it did not.[8]

[5] John Maynard Keynes, *The General Theory of Employment, Interest and Money* (New York: Harcourt, Brace & Co., 1936), pp. 3n, 4–22.

[6] J. R. Hicks, "Mr. Keynes and the Classics," *Econometrica*, April 1937, p. 147.

[7] Keynes, *General Theory*, pp. 29, 289, 296.

[8] For example, Henry Thornton, *An Enquiry into the Nature and Effects of the Paper Credit of Great Britain*, ed. F. A. v. Hayek (New York: Augustus M. Kelley, 1965), pp. 96–97, 232–233; David Ricardo, *The Works and Correspondence of David Ricardo*, ed. Piero Sraffa (Cambridge: Cambridge Uni-

Since the two classic definitions of classical economics, by Marx and by Keynes, are both so idiosyncratic, some other basis must be sought for the general usage of the term. There is something honorific, as well as indicative of certain doctrines and approaches, in the term "classical" economics. It connotes the giants of the field—Adam Smith and Ricardo, but not Harriet Martineau or Jane Marcet, who popularized the same doctrines and who may have directly reached a wider audience than the more illustrious economists. In economics, as elsewhere, "classical" usually implies something that has established an authoritative tradition that serves as a point of departure for later developments in the same field. In this sense, Adam Smith can be said to have founded classical economics, even if many (or all) of his concepts and theories can be found scattered through the works of numerous predecessors who left no disciples and founded no enduring school.

Since the authoritative tradition that built upon *The Wealth of Nations* underwent a major change with the marginalist revolution of the 1870s, the end points of classical economics can be reasonably well established, about one hundred years apart. Within that span, there were three men who were clearly classical in every sense: Adam Smith, David Ricardo, and John Stuart Mill. There were others as fully part of the same tradition, though not of equal stature, James Mill and J. R. McCulloch being the best representatives of this group.

---

versity Press, 1951–55), III, 90; Alfred Marshall, *Official Papers* (London: Macmillan & Co., 1926), pp. 267–268; Irving Fisher, *The Purchasing Power of Money* (New York: Augustus M. Kelley, 1963), pp. 159–160.

There were still others who contributed key concepts to classical economics without sharing all of its methods and conclusions: J. B. Say, whose law was embedded in classical tradition, but who opposed the classical theory of value; T. R. Malthus, whose population theory held a central position in classical economics, but who was a leading dissenter on value theory and on Say's Law; and Sir Edward West, who shared with Malthus the development of the law of diminishing returns and the "Ricardian" rent theory,[9] but did not join in the general development of classical economics. There were other economists who did not make contributions of this magnitude, but who shared with Say and Malthus the characteristic of being classical in some respects but not in others: Robert Torrens, Nassau Senior, and Karl Marx being prominent among these. In short, the classical economists were not a clearly defined set of economists, but a certain small solid core shading off into a larger penumbra, which was an essential part of the overall phenomenon, since classical economics includes fundamental ideas which did not originate with those who were classical economists in all respects.

The criticisms of classical economics by contemporaries and by later interpreters can be divided into (1) criticisms of the philosophy underlying classical approaches and conclusions, and (2) criticisms of the substantive economic analysis that constitutes classical economics. The philosophic criticisms include criticisms of methodology as well as criticisms of social values and the general classical moral and behavioral theories. The

[9] Ricardo himself credited Malthus and West with priority. Ricardo, *Works*, 1, 5.

positive economic propositions criticized included all the major propositions of classical economics: the labor theory of value, Say's Law, the Malthusian population theory, and the quantity theory of money.

Classical social philosophy will be discussed in this first chapter, then classical macroeconomics and microeconomics, and finally the classical analysis of the scope and method of economics.

The "Conservatism" of the Classical Economists

The classical economists are often depicted as defenders of the status quo, apologists for the socioeconomic powers (and practices) that be, and as believers in a "natural harmony" which makes deliberate intervention in the economy unnecessary and detrimental. Sometimes they are excused because the "simpler" conditions of their time were more in accord with their theories than are the "complexities" of our time. Of course, there is not a shred of evidence that eighteenth-century or nineteenth-century society was any simpler than twentieth-century society, though undoubtedly our *knowledge* of the complexities of other ages is often primitive and shallow. Moreover, the notion that laissez-faire economics originated in a laissez-faire world[10] is grotesque.

Transfer versus Production of Wealth

Mercantilism was still the dominant theory and practice when Adam Smith's *The Wealth of Nations* appeared in 1776, though it was an orthodoxy already under attack theoretically and beginning to crumble in practice. The

[10] As suggested in Robert L. Heilbroner, *The Worldly Philosophers* (New York: Simon & Schuster, 1961), p. 42.

8

mercantilists still promoted and supported an enormous array of detailed economic controls designed to produce an export surplus, largely at the expense of the lower classes, by keeping labor cheap so as to undersell foreigners in the international market while still permitting substantial profits to domestic merchants and manufacturers. Adam Smith opposed the mercantilists, not simply on policy, but on such basic concepts as the meaning of "wealth" and the meaning of "nation."

The mercantilists conceived of wealth in *competitive* terms, as something taken by one from another, an inherently differential gain, like winning a race.[11] It was *only* "the demand of strangers" which could increase the wealth of a nation, according to mercantilist doctrine.[12] Wealth being gold, which is obtainable by an export surplus, riches "are forbid to all countries which have neither mines, or foreign trade."[13] It is only "the treasure which is brought to the Realm by the ballance of our foreign trade" which constitutes the amount "by which we are enriched."[14] The government was repeatedly invoked to advance the economic interests of society "at the expense of other societies."[15] The cardinal rule of mercantilism was "to sell more to strangers yearly than we consume of theirs in value."[16] By the same token, a nation must try to produce at home, instead of buying

[11] Sir James Steuart, *Works*, Vol. 1, *An Inquiry into the Principles of Political Economy* (London: T. Cadell, 1805 [originally 1767]), 310–312.

[12] Ibid., pp. 313–314. [13] Ibid., pp. 326–327.

[14] Thomas Mun, *England's Treasure by Forraign Trade* (New York: Augustus M. Kelley, 1965 [originally 1664]), p. 21.

[15] Steuart, *Works*, I, 347; see also p. 360.

[16] Mun, *England's Treasure*, p. 5.

abroad, "things which now we fetch from strangers to our great impoverishing."[17]

From the mercantilist point of view, not only an export surplus but also the repression of wages, the promotion of imperialism and even slavery could be seen as natural corollaries to the pursuit of wealth by the propertied classes which constituted the nation. With the nation conceived of as only *part* of its population, it was possible to speak of "a whole nation fed and provided for gratuitously"[18] under slavery.

Adam Smith's conception of the nation was implicit in his statement that "no society can be flourishing and happy, of which the far greater part of the members are poor and miserable."[19] This seems so obvious today only because society or the nation is implicitly conceived of as coextensive with its population—a view by no means universally accepted by Smith's contemporaries in Europe or in America. Even a century later, John Stuart Mill could say, "When they say country, read aristocracy, and you will never be far from the truth."[20]

For Smith and later classical economists, wealth was conceived of not as a stock of money but as a flow of goods—"real income" in modern terminology.[21] Smith rejected the view "which represents national wealth as consisting in the abundance, and national poverty in the scarcity, of gold and silver."[22] More fundamentally, Smith

[17] Ibid., p. 7.   [18] Steuart, *Works*, I, 337.
[19] Adam Smith, *An Inquiry into the Nature and Causes of the Wealth of Nations* (New York: Modern Library, 1937), p. 79.
[20] John Stuart Mill, "Speech on the British Constitution," *Autobiography* (London: Oxford University Press, 1949), p. 276.
[21] Smith, *Wealth of Nations*, pp. lx, 321, 419.
[22] Ibid., p. 238.

and the classical school stressed the *creation* of wealth, rather than its *transfer*. International trade was seen as a source of mutual benefit, rather than of differential gain, since it led to a larger and cheaper aggregate output.[23] Both imperialism and slavery were regarded as *losing* ventures, for they inhibited the creation of wealth while concentrating on its appropriation. The classical economists saw the gains from imperialism going to a small class of wealthy businessmen and colonial officials to be greatly outweighed by the costs paid by the taxpayers to maintain an empire. Adam Smith declared that "great fleets and armies . . . acquire nothing which can compensate the expense of maintaining them."[24] The interference of the mother country with the colonies' economies inhibited the latter's economic development,[25] but without a corresponding gain to the mother country, except in terms of national glory. The loss of one was not the gain of the other, for the aggregate output between them was reduced below what it would otherwise be. *The Wealth of Nations* closed with the observation that "it is surely time that Great Britain should free herself from the expense of defending those provinces in time of war, and of supporting any part of their civil or military establishments in time of peace, and endeavor to accom-

[23] Ibid., p. 415; Ricardo, *Works*, I, 133–134; John Stuart Mill, *Principles of Political Economy*, ed. W. J. Ashley (London: Longmans, Green and Co., 1909), pp 580–581. This edition of Mill's *Principles* is cited hereafter as "Ashley Edition." In the variorum edition published by the University of Toronto Press, cited hereafter as "Toronto Edition," the *Principles* constitute volumes II and III of the *Collected Works* (Toronto: University of Toronto Press, 1965), pp. 592–593.

[24] Smith, *Wealth of Nations*, p. 325.

[25] Ibid., p. 559.

modate her future views and designs to the real medi-
ocrity of her circumstances."[26]

Adam Smith could not have felt that this rational ad-
vice would be heeded, for he had observed earlier:

No nation ever voluntarily gave up the dominion of
any province, how troublesome soever it might be to
govern it, and how small soever the revenue which it
afforded might be in proportion to the expense which
it occasioned. Such sacrifices, though they might fre-
quently be agreeable to the interest, are always morti-
fying to the pride of every nation, and what is perhaps
of still greater consequence, they are always contrary
to the private interest of the governing part of it, who
would thereby be deprived of the disposal of many
places of trust and profit, of many opportunities of
acquiring wealth and distinction, which the possession
of the most turbulent, and to the great body of the
people, the most unprofitable province seldom fails to
afford.[27]

Similar reasoning later led James Mill to regard the
British Empire as an elaborate government make-work
project, "a vast system of outdoor relief for the upper
classes."[28] Ricardo saw theoretical possibilities for a nation as a whole to benefit economically at the expense of
its colonies,[29] but did not argue that this had in fact happened generally.

Slavery was attacked not only in moral terms but in
economic terms by the classical economists. Its key eco-

[26] Ibid., p. 900. [27] Ibid., p. 582.
[28] James Mill quoted in J. A. Hobson, *Imperialism* (Ann
Arbor: University of Michigan Press, 1965), p. 51.
[29] Ricardo, *Works*, I, Chap. xxv.

nomic weakness was the absence of the incentive of self-interest by the worker. Although the maintenance costs of slaves were lower than the rate of pay of free workers, the labor costs of getting a given amount of work done with slaves was often higher.[30] Though "work done by slaves . . . appears to cost only their maintenance" said Adam Smith, it is "in the end the dearest of any."[31] It was man's "pride," which "makes him love to domineer," rather than the economics of the situation, which explained the persistence of slavery for Smith.[32] Ricardo did not analyze the economics of slavery, though he did express his shame at being part of a nation that permitted it.[33] John Stuart Mill argued morally against slavery[34] and, as an economist, followed the classical tradition by pronouncing it "inefficient and unproductive," due to its limited incentives.[35] Mill, however, was not nearly as confident as Smith had been that slavery was so unprofitable to the individual slave owner that only psychological reasons could explain its persistence. Mill sharply separated the question of the profitability of slavery to slave owners from the larger question of the economic effect of slavery on "the community,"[36] which was considered largely negative.

The most thorough application of classical economic analysis to slavery was *The Slave Power* by John Elliot

[30] Smith, *Wealth of Nations*, pp. 80–81.

[31] Ibid., p. 365.   [32] Ibid., p. 365.

[33] Ricardo, *Works*, v, 483.

[34] See Michael St. John Packe, *The Life of John Stuart Mill* (New York: Macmillan Co., 1959), pp. 423–427.

[35] J. S. Mill, *Principles*, Ashley edn., p. 251; Toronto edn., p. 247.

[36] Ibid., Ashley edn., p. 253; Toronto edn., p. 249.

Cairnes, a disciple of Mill and often considered the last of the classical economists. Cairnes systematically traced the economic and social consequences of slavery, including (1) the exhaustion of the soil by a work force whose incentives were insufficient to produce a varied knowledge and application of agricultural techniques,[37] (2) the desperate need for territorial expansion by a slaveholding community to replace its own successively exhausted soils,[38] and (3) the external cost of slavery in generating attitudes inimical to economic progress in the general free population.[39] His was the most systematic application to slavery of the classical approach, which viewed the creation of wealth as central, in contrast to the mercantilistic emphasis on its appropriation or transfer.[40]

Political Classes

In addition to opposing such major contemporary institutions as imperialism and slavery, the classical economists attacked the dominant social classes of the time: the landed aristocracy, the rising capitalists, and the political powers that be. A recurring theme in *The Wealth of Nations* was "the clamour and sophistry of merchants and manufacturers,"[41] whose "mean rapacity" and

[37] John E. Cairnes, *The Slave Power* (New York: Harper & Row, 1969 [originally 1862]), pp. 55–56.

[38] Ibid., pp. 62, 180.

[39] Ibid., pp. 81–83, 143–144, 147–148, 176–177.

[40] Ironically, the *analytic* approach of the mercantilists has been revived in the theories and policies of modern groups with radically different social philosophies. See Thomas Sowell, "Economics and Black People," *Review of Black Political Economy*, Winter-Spring 1971, pp. 14–16.

[41] Smith, *Wealth of Nations*, p. 128; see also pp. 249–250, 402–403, 429, 438, 579.

"monopolizing spirit"[42] led them "on many occasions" to "deceive and even to oppress the public."[43] These were people who "seldom meet together, even for merriment and diversion, but the conversation ends in a conspiracy against the public, or in some contrivance to raise prices."[44] In contrast to the exalted role of "the statesman" in mercantilist literature,[45] Adam Smith referred to "that insidious and crafty animal, vulgarly called a statesman or politician, whose councils are directed to the momentary fluctuation of affairs."[46] Political leaders were not only careless of the public's long-run interests but extravagant with its tax money:

It is the highest impertinence and presumption, therefore, in kings and ministers, to pretend to watch over the economy of private people, and to restrain their expense, either by sumptuary laws, or by prohibiting the importation of foreign luxuries. They are themselves always, and without any exception, the greatest spendthrifts in the society. Let them look well after their own expense, and they may safely trust private people with theirs. If their own extravagance does not ruin the state, that of their subjects never will.[47]

[42] Ibid., p. 460. [43] Ibid., p. 250. [44] Ibid., p. 128.
[45] "It is the business of a statesman to judge of the expediency of different schemes of œconomy, and by degrees to model the minds of his subjects so as to induce them, from the allurement of private interest, to cooperate in the execution of his plan" (Steuart, *Works*, I, 4); ". . . nothing is impossible to an able statesman" (p. 15); the statesman is "constantly awake" on economic matters (p. 73), as the "great genius of Mr. de Colbert" and the "genius of Mr. Law" show them to be "born statesmen" (p. 88).
[46] Smith, *Wealth of Nations*, p. 435; see also p. 329.
[47] Loc. cit.

Landlords were regarded by Smith as well meaning on the whole, though easily taken in by businessmen,[48] but landlords were passive beneficiaries of progress[49] and "love to reap where they never sowed."[50] If the landlord got off relatively lightly in Smith, he was the chief villain of the Ricardian school. Landlords grew richer "in their sleep, without working, risking or economizing,"[51] their income being the price exacted for their "consent" for the use of land, a consent made necessary solely "by the arrangements of society,"[52] a legalized "tribute"[53] paid to someone who is "merely a sinecurist" quartered on the land.[54] The great political crusade of the Ricardians was the repeal of the Corn Laws, which kept wheat prices artificially high to benefit the landed interests.

Capitalists were considered more useful, but no more appealing, at least not to John Stuart Mill, who said: "I confess I am not charmed with the ideal of life held out by those who think that the normal state of human beings is that of struggling to get on; that the trampling, crushing, elbowing, and treading on each other's heels, which form the existing type of social life, are the most desirable lot of humankind, or anything but the disagreeable symptoms of one of the phases of industrial progress."[55]

One of the most ill-founded charges against the classical economists is that they believed in a natural "harmony

[48] Ibid., pp. 249, 250.　　　　[49] Ibid., p. 247.
[50] Ibid., p. 49.
[51] J. S. Mill, *Principles*, Ashley edn., p. 818; Toronto edn., pp. 819–820.
[52] Ibid., Ashley edn., p. 422; Toronto edn., p. 416.
[53] Ibid., Ashley edn., p. 429; Toronto edn., p. 423.
[54] Ibid., Ashley edn., p. 231; Toronto edn., p. 228.
[55] Ibid., Ashley edn., p. 748; Toronto edn., p. 754.

16

of interests" among the various social classes. Certainly the classical economists did not regard social classes as subjectively harmonious nor the political rulers as a harmonizing influence. The laissez-faire doctrine of the classical economists was based on the hope and belief that *conflict*—economic competition—within a suitable institutional framework would lead to the best allocation of resources. It was not "benevolence" but "their own interest" which caused people to serve each other, according to Smith.[56] The famous "contradiction" between the "sympathy" which was central to Adam Smith's *The Theory of Moral Sentiments* in 1759 and the "self-interest" which was central to his *The Wealth of Nations* in 1776 is more apparent than real. It is one thing to explain how we derive our moral sentiments and quite another to explain economic behavior, which is only partially affected by moral sentiments. The shift of topics between the two books was not a change of mind. *The Theory of Moral Sentiments* itself had regarded beneficence as "less essential to society than justice," without which society "must in a moment crumble into atoms."[57] It was the artificial maintenance of some system of justice—*indirectly* derived from sympathy—and not any "natural harmony" among men which made possible the existence of society, even "without any mutual love and affection . . . by a mercenary exchange of good offices according to an agreed evaluation."[58]

The supposed "harmony of interests" in Adam Smith has often been interpreted to mean that the optimum

[56] Smith, *Wealth of Nations*, p. 14.
[57] Adam Smith, *The Theory of Moral Sentiments*, Pt. II, Sec. II, Chap. VI, p. 98.
[58] Smith, *Theory of Moral Sentiments*, pp. 97–98.

situation for society is simply the aggregation of individual optimum situations—ignoring mutual interdependence and committing the fallacy of composition. But Smith never advanced such a doctrine, and his famous reference to an "invisible hand," which leads the individual self-seeker "to promote an end which was no part of his intention,"[59] suggests that he did distinguish individual benefit from social benefit conceptually, advancing a *behavioral theory* that the former promoted the latter (by its effect on resource allocation), not a conceptual *identity* that simply defined the latter as the summation of the former. Private and social economic interests coincided in an uncontrolled market "in ordinary cases,"[60] not by definition. In cases where externalities were involved, Smith was prepared to agree even to "a manifest violation" of natural liberty when "the natural liberty of a few individuals" endangered society at large—not only in such things as fire regulations but also in certain banking regulations as well.[61]

The emphasis of the Ricardian school on the distribution of income by social class certainly was not one which exemplified any "harmony of interests." In Ricardo, as in Smith, the landlord gained in the long run at the expense of capitalists and workers,[62] and, in addition, wages and profits—in Ricardo's peculiar definitions—always moved inversely to one another.[63] John Stuart Mill found the distribution of income anything but harmonious, "the largest portions" going to "those who have never worked

[59] Smith, *Wealth of Nations*, p. 423.
[60] Ibid., p. 594.   [61] Ibid., p. 308.
[62] Ibid., p. 247–248; Ricardo, *Works*, I, 83, 125, 335–336, 337.
[63] Ricardo, *Works*, I, 27, 35, 110, 115, 118, 132, 159, 205, 214, 215, 226, 289, 296, 323, 333, 404n, 411.

at all, the next largest to those whose work is almost
nominal, and so in a descending scale, the remuneration
dwindling as the work grows harder and more disagreeable, until the most fatiguing and exhausting bodily labour cannot count with certainty on being able to earn
the necessaries of life."[64] Even J. B. Say, sometimes depicted as an apologist for the status quo, was in fact quite
critical of existing conditions:

> . . . in countries said to be in a flourishing condition,
> how many human beings can be enumerated, in a situa-
> tion to partake of such enjoyments? One out of a hun-
> dred thousand at most; and out of a thousand, perhaps
> not one who may be permitted to enjoy what is called
> a comfortable independence. The haggardness of pov-
> erty is everywhere seen contrasted with the sleekness
> of wealth, the extorted labour of some compensating
> for the idleness of others, wretched hovels by the side
> of stately colonnades, the rags of indigence blended
> with the ensigns of opulence; in a word, the most use-
> less profusion in the midst of the most urgent wants.
>
> Persons, who under a vicious order of things have
> obtained a competent share of social enjoyments, are
> never in want of arguments to justify to the eye of
> reason such a state of society; for what may not ad-
> mit of apology when exhibited in but one point of
> view? If the same individuals were to-morrow required
> to cast anew the lots assigning them a place in society,
> they would find many things to object to.[65]

[64] J. S. Mill, *Principles*, Ashley edn., p. 208; Toronto edn.,
p. 207.
[65] Jean-Baptiste Say, *A Treatise on Political Economy*, trans.
by Clement C. Biddle (Philadelphia: Grigg & Elliot, 1834), p.
liii.

To say that the classical economists were not advocates of "natural harmony" doctrines is not to deny that such doctrines flourished in the classical period or that classical theories were used by popularizers of such doctrines. Bastiat's *Harmonies économiques* in 1850 was perhaps the most famous, though by no means the sole, example of this genre. Richard Cobden, Jane Marcet, Harriet Martineau, and numerous others preached social harmony, as to some extent did T. R. Malthus, who had one foot in the classical tradition and one foot outside. The classical economists cannot be blamed for the uses made of their doctrines, and in at least one case—John Stuart Mill reviewing Harriet Martineau—there was a public repudiation of these social apologetics.[66] Indeed, one of the distinguishing features of classical economics, which Marx contrasted with later "vulgar economics," was that the classical economists had openly discussed "the economic bases of the different classes" and their "ever-growing antagonism."[67]

The Market

Although the classical economists favored the conduct of economic activity through market processes rather than political processes, it should not be supposed that they found the market perfect. The classical economists recognized the existence of monopolies, and in fact used the term "monopoly" very broadly to include many forms of market imperfection or inelastic supply, as in

[66] John Stuart Mill, "Miss Martineau's Summary of Political Economy," *Monthly Repository*, May 1834, pp. 318–322.

[67] Karl Marx and Frederick Engels, *Selected Correspondence* (New York: International Publishers, 1942), p. 57; see also Marx, *Capital*, I, 17–18.

the "monopoly" of land.[68] Adam Smith saw the effect of a monopoly as "keeping the market constantly understocked"[69] and reducing the efficiency of management, which requires highly competitive markets to force everyone to be efficient in "self-defense."[70] Monopolies cause "the whole annual produce of the land and labour" to be "less than they would otherwise be"[71] because they "derange more or less the natural distribution of the stock of society."[72] In addition, Smith recognized the external social costs of the division of labor, which demoralized the worker who performed simple, repetitive tasks, and advocated publicly subsidized schooling—not to be general in England for another century—to offset this.[73] Ricardo (and his contemporary disciples) formally analyzed a model of perfect competition, though noting in *ad hoc* fashion the existence of monopoly, defined as inelastic supply.[74] John Stuart Mill went beyond the simple dichotomy of competition and monopoly to suggest modifications of traditional competitive results due to social mores, even in markets not structurally noncompetitive.[75]

The classical economists were not rigidly opposed to all government intervention in the market. Smith's "natural liberty" and laissez-faire principle was never a dogma.[76] The classical economists not only accepted cer-

[68] J. S. Mill, *Principles*, Ashley edn., p. 235; Toronto edn., p. 232.
[69] Smith, *Wealth of Nations*, p. 61.
[70] Ibid., p. 14.   [71] Ibid., p. 574.
[72] Ibid., p. 596.   [73] Ibid., pp. 734, 737–740.
[74] Ricardo, *Works*, I, 249–250, 385.
[75] J. S. Mill, *Principles*, Bk. II, Chap. IV, Ashley edn.; Toronto edn.
[76] Jacob Viner, "Adam Smith and Laissez-Faire," *Journal of Political Economy*, April 1927, pp. 198–232.

tain intervention in the market, they suggested some themselves. Adam Smith wanted highway toll charges to be so arranged that the luxuries of the rich would subsidize the shipment of the necessities of the poor.[77] He also wanted a tax system which would be somewhat progressive and redistributive,[78] based on the ability-to-pay principle.[79] John Stuart Mill advocated public subsidy of emigration by the poor.[80]

While classical economists neither asserted the perfection of the market nor denied any possible beneficial role to government intervention in the economy, they were steadfast in their *general* policy of laissez-faire, in part precisely because of the *dis*harmony of interests and the dangers to the public when organized private groups influenced government economic policy. Adam Smith said:

> . . . the monopoly which our manufacturers have obtained . . . has so much increased the number of some particular tribes of them, that, like an overgrown standing army, they have become formidable to the government, and upon many occasions intimidate the legislature. The member of Parliament who supports every proposal for strengthening this monopoly, is sure to acquire not only the reputation of understanding trade, but great popularity and influence with an order of men whose numbers and wealth render them of great importance. If he opposes them, on the contrary, and still more if he has authority enough to be able to thwart them, neither the most acknowledged probity,

[77] Smith, *Wealth of Nations*, p. 683.
[78] Ibid., p. 794.   [79] Ibid., p. 777.
[80] J. S. Mill, *Principles*, Ashley edn., pp. 381–383; Toronto edn., pp. 376–378.

nor the highest rank, nor the greatest public services, can protect him from the most infamous abuse and detraction, from personal insults, nor sometimes from real danger, arising from the insolent outrage of furious and disappointed monopolists.[81]

To Smith, government intervention in the economy was conceived of as intervention on behalf of the wealthy and powerful—as it was overwhelmingly in his day, and as it still is to a greater extent than popularly assumed, even today.

By the time of John Stuart Mill, it was at least widely believed that government intervention in the economy on behalf of the poor was a real prospect, so that Mill criticized "impatient reformers, thinking it easier to get possession of the government than of the intellects and dispositions of the public," such reformers being "under a constant temptation" to expand "the province of government."[82] Mill declared that laissez-faire "should be the general practice" and "every departure from it, unless required by some great good, is a certain evil."[83] This was not only because governments tended to be inefficient,[84] but because democratic government readily becomes a vehicle by which intolerant majorities can impose their standards and tastes on individuals,[85] and because the spread of government economic activity was also the spread of its extralegal influence,[86] including its ideolog-

[81] Smith, *Wealth of Nations*, p. 438.

[82] J. S. Mill, *Principles*, Ashley edn., p. 795; Toronto edn., p. 799.

[83] Ibid., Ashley edn., p. 950; Toronto edn., p. 945.

[84] Ibid., Ashley edn., p. 947; Toronto edn., p. 941.

[85] Ibid., Ashley edn., p. 945; Toronto edn., pp. 939–940.

[86] Ibid., Ashley edn., p. 961; Toronto edn., p. 955.

ical influence on education[87] and its seductive opportunities for important jobs.[88]

The classical economists were profoundly mistrustful of all governments. Ricardo considered it "salutary" that government action should be constrained by a certain "dread of insurrection,"[89] though he had no desire to see actual insurrection and promoted reform as "the most efficacious preventative of Revolution."[90]

Wars

In addition to attacking the most powerful classes, institutions, and philosophies of their time, the classical economists opposed the contemporary wars in which their countries were engaged or were being urged to engage. Smith's *The Wealth of Nations* appeared in the year of the American Declaration of Independence from Great Britain, and his analysis of that conflict led him to suggest either a negotiated peace or a unilateral withdrawal by his own country.[91] During the Napoleonic Wars, James Mill urged a negotiated peace,[92] though powerful forces were in favor of a policy of fighting on to total victory, as of course Britain did. The elder Mill declared that "war is the greatest calamity with which a nation can be visited."[93] In a later era, John Stuart Mill was to say of a

[87] Ibid., Ashley edn., p. 956; Toronto edn., p. 950.

[88] Ibid., Ashley edn., p. 949; Toronto edn., p. 943.

[89] Ricardo, *Works*, VII, 241; He also said, "A government is free in proportion to the ease with which the people can overthrow it." Ibid., VIII, 133.

[90] Ibid., VIII, 49.

[91] Smith, *Wealth of Nations*, pp. 581–582.

[92] James Mill, *Commerce Defended* (London: C. & R. Baldwin, 1808), p. 128.

[93] Ibid., p. 130.

British military leader and hero, "every feather in his cap has cost the nation more than he and his whole lineage would fetch if they were sold for lumber."[94] J. B. Say expressed similar disgust with the "military fanaticism" of Napoleon.[95]

The classical economists were less naïve than some modern opponents of war. Wars were not seen as simply the work of evil men who imposed them on "the people," but as popularly supported adventures. Adam Smith said:

In great empires the people who live in the capital, and in the provinces remote from the scene of action, feel, many of them, scarce any inconveniency from the war; but enjoy, at their ease, the amusement of reading in the newspapers the exploits of their own fleets and armies. To them this amusement compensates the small difference between the taxes which they pay on account of the war, and those which they had been accustomed to pay in time of peace. They are commonly dissatisfied with the return of peace, which puts an end to their amusement, and to a thousand visionary hopes of conquest and national glory, from a longer continuance of the war.[96]

Smith urged that wars not be financed by government deficits but by pay-as-you-go taxation, so that the full economic cost should be clearly visible and personally felt by everyone.[97] Were this policy followed, wars "would in general be more speedily concluded and less

[94] J. S. Mill, "Speech on the British Constitution," *Autobiography*, p. 278.

[95] Jean-Baptiste Say, *Œuvres diverses de J.-B. Say* (Paris: Guillauminet et Cie, 1848), p. 397.

[96] Smith, *Wealth of Nations*, p. 872.

[97] Ibid., p. 878.

wantonly undertaken."[98] Ricardo opposed the creation of a special fund to retire the national debt on grounds that it was sure to be diverted to military adventures: "While ministers have this fund virtually at their disposal they will on the slightest occasion be disposed for war. To keep them peaceable you must keep them poor."[99]

The classical economists were not pacifists,[100] but were simply critical of the wars of their time and of the recklessness with which wars have been undertaken throughout history. Opposition to war in general is much easier than opposition to the particular current wars supported by one's fellow countrymen, but the classical economists boldly opposed both.

THE PRACTICAL BEHAVIOR OF THE CLASSICAL ECONOMISTS

The classical economists were men of affairs as well as theorists, and their actual behavior in the struggles of their times provides additional evidence on their underlying values and convictions.

One fact stands out clearly: the classical economists were not activated by personal self-interest in the things they advocated. Adam Smith, who achieved financial security from an annuity paid for tutoring a young nobleman on a tour of the continent, declared this method of acquiring an education "absurd" in *The Wealth of Nations*.[101] He also denounced the indolence, irresponsibility, and logrolling in his own profession as an

[98] Loc. cit.　　　　　　[99] Ricardo, *Works*, IX, 180.
[100] Smith, *Wealth of Nations*, pp. 738–739; Alexander Bain, *James Mill* (London: Longmans, Green, and Co., 1882), p. 49; Packe, *Life of John Stuart Mill*, p. 424.
[101] Smith, *Wealth of Nations*, p. 728.

26

academician.[102] Contrary to prevailing practice, he insisted on returning students' fees when he had to be absent.[103] Ricardo's economics and his speeches in Parliament attacked the landed interests more severely than any other, though he was himself a large landholder. This pattern was typical of Ricardo's whole career:

When a Bank proprietor, he argued strenuously and warmly against the inordinate gains of that body; he defended the cause of the fund-holders when he had ceased to be one; he was accused of an attempt to ruin the landed interest after he became a large landed proprietor; and while a member of Parliament, he advocated the cause of reform, which, if adopted, would have deprived him of his seat.[104]

Personal pecuniary self-interest was by no means a dominating characteristic of the classical economists. Adam Smith gave away "large sums" in secret acts of charity, "much beyond what would have been expected from his fortune."[105] Ricardo also secretly offered and gave aid to friends in financial distress.[106] Henry Thornton, the leading monetary theorist of the classical period, provided the money for Hannah More's schools for the poor for 25 years,[107] and before his marriage gave away

[102] Ibid., pp. 717–720.
[103] Francis W. Hirst, *Adam Smith* (New York: Macmillan Co., 1904), pp. 115–116; John Rae, *The Life of Adam Smith* (London: Macmillan & Co., 1895), pp. 167–168, 170–171.
[104] Ricardo, *Works*, x, 13.
[105] Rae, *Life of Adam Smith*, p. 437.
[106] Ricardo, *Works*, VI, 122; ibid., x, 113, 118, 131, 133.
[107] F. A. v. Hayek, "Introduction," Thornton, *Paper Credit of Great Britain*, p. 23.

six-sevenths of his annual income to charity.[108] Nassau Senior, holder of the first chair in political economy, went into teaching at a salary no more than one-fifth what he had been earning in nonacademic pursuits.[109] John Stuart Mill "gave money freely," sometimes to organized charities and sometimes to poor people he simply encountered on the streets.[110]

Malthus, who usually defended landlords, was no landlord himself. Malthus was a far more conservative figure than Adam Smith or the Ricardians. So were Lauderdale and Chalmers, who, together with Malthus, were the major figures in the British school of dissenters from Say's Law. If Malthus is to be regarded as classical, then he must be held responsible for a highly conservative image which he generalized to those more centrally classical economists who took very different positions from him on most social and political issues. It is doubtful whether the general public carefully distinguished the different schools of economists, since political economy was a new phenomenon in itself, and educated opinion in the early nineteenth century tended to be divided for and against the whole field. Certainly such popular writers as William Cobbett lumped Ricardo, Malthus, and others together for a general condemnation, and his approach could not have been unique, for Walter Bagehot observed that "no real Englishman in his secret soul was ever sorry for the death of a political economist."[111]

[108] Ibid., p. 25.
[109] Richard Whately, *Introductory Lectures on Political Economy*, 2nd edn. (London: B. Fellowes, 1832), p. 2.
[110] Packe, *Life of John Stuart Mill*, p. 484.
[111] Quoted in Jacob Viner, "The Economist in History," *American Economic Review*, May 1963, p. 13.

One of the real crusades of the classical period was the drive to repeal the Combination Laws which had effectively outlawed labor unions as conspiracies. Adam Smith had alluded to the partiality of such laws, which left workingmen at the mercy of "combinations" of employers who are in "a sort of tacit, but constant and uniform combination, not to raise the wages of labour."[112] Francis Place, a Benthamite in politics and in economics a disciple of Ricardo and James Mill, spearheaded the drive.[113] He was aided by McCulloch,[114] who was encouraged by Ricardo, who termed such laws "unjust and oppressive to the working classes."[115] James Mill joined "heartily" in Francis Place's drive for schools for the poor,[116] and John Stuart Mill, as a young man, was arrested with Place for handing out birth control leaflets in a working-class neighborhood.[117] Even Malthus supported child labor laws.[118]

The central figures in classical economics promoted or supported many specific reforms in their own times, most of these reforms being aimed at aiding the working class or the poor generally. However, some reforms with similar aims were opposed by the classical economists, as conflicting with specific classical doctrines—notably the Malthusian population theory. Moreover, some classical economists or disciples were more reform-oriented than others—as was true among their nonclassical contempo-

[112] Smith, *Wealth of Nations*, pp. 66–67.
[113] Graham Wallas, *The Life of Francis Place* (New York: Burt Franklin, 1951), Chap. VIII.
[114] Ibid., pp. 206–207.   [115] Ricardo, *Works*, VIII, 316.
[116] Wallas, *Life of Francis Place*, p. 99.
[117] Packe, *Life of John Stuart Mill*, pp. 57–58.
[118] Mark Blaug, *Ricardian Economics* (New Haven: Yale University Press, 1958), p. 196.

raries, such as Nassau Senior.[119] There was, in short, no rigid doctrinaire position on social policy in general or on the specific issues of the day.

SUMMARY

The classical economists can hardly be considered conservative in terms of a favorable predisposition toward existing institutions or the dominant social classes. Adam Smith's attacks on both were sweeping, and the Ricardians were active in attacking not only economic anachronisms (the Corn Laws, prohibitions against trade unions and other mercantilistic regulations) but were also active—as Benthamites[120]—in attacks on political relics and abuses.[121]

The rise of more radical critics, schools, and movements with the development of industrial capitalism made the classical economists seem more conservative. Moreover, the rallying cry, *laissez-faire!* was, in the new context, no longer simply an attack on institutional favoritism to the upper classes. It was now usable as a defense of new vested interests who were imposing important external costs on society by unsanitary working and living conditions, child labor, pollution, etc. The classical economists themselves were not inclined to use their doctrines in this way, and in fact favored some legislation aimed at the abuses of industrialism and urbanism.[122]

[119] Marian Bowley, *Nassau Senior and Classical Economics* (London: George Allen & Unwin, 1937), Pt. II.
[120] Elie Halevy, *The Growth of Philosophic Radicalism* (New York: Kelley & Millman, n.d.), Pt. III.
[121] Wallas, *Life of Francis Place*, p. 161.
[122] J. A. Schumpeter, *History of Economic Analysis* (New York: Oxford University Press, 1951), p. 402.

However, they were constrained to some extent by their general tradition of laissez-faire as well as by the implications of their economic theories.

The Malthusian population theory made all kinds of income-transfer policies appear futile as a means of helping the poor, and raised the specter of all of society being dragged down to the poverty level if they attempted directly to raise the poor above it.[123] Say's Law, together with the comparative statics, long-run equilibrium of the Ricardians, made unemployment a transitory phenomenon growing out of passing maladjustments and government interferences. Aggregate disequilibrium and wage inflexibilities were both rejected by the Ricardians.[124]

Whether the conservative elements in a given school of thought arise from predisposition or from the implications of certain analysis may matter little from some points of view. But it matters considerably in assessing claims that ideas in general (or economic theories in particular) are rationalizations of socially determined predispositions,[125] which can be treated as "modern" or "outmoded" instead of being analyzed in terms of their logical and empirical validity.

The really savage comments of the classical economists were all directed toward the powers that be. Their criticisms of more radical thinkers tended to be more in sorrow than in anger. Ricardo's references to Robert Owen were laudatory as to his intentions and character,[126] and

[123] Ricardo, *Works*, I, 108.

[124] Thomas Sowell, *Say's Law: An Historical Analysis* (Princeton: Princeton University Press, 1972), pp. 20, 126–127.

[125] See Max Lerner, "Introduction," Adam Smith, *Wealth of Nations*, pp. ix–x.

[126] Ricardo, *Works*, v, 467–468.

he had similarly high regard for the character of Sismondi,[127] though he rejected the specific analyses and policies of both men. John Stuart Mill's analyses of socialist thought were very similar in this respect.[128] Even as conservative an economist as Malthus never impugned the motives of such revolutionary thinkers as Godwin and Condorcet.

One of the curious facts about the classical economists is that most of them were members of minority groups—minorities not simply in some numerical sense, but in ways that were socially relevant. Being a Scotsman was not an incidental fact in the England of Adam Smith's day, as he discovered in his youth from his fellow students and the Oxford University administration.[129] In later life he wrote back to Oxford to complain about continuing discrimination against Scottish students, and on another occasion he warned his friend and compatriot David Hume that "the whole wise English nation . . . will love to mortify a Scotchman."[130] Malthus, the two Mills, and J. R. McCulloch were also Scottish. David Ricardo was of Jewish ancestry and Jean-Baptiste Say was descended from Huguenots who had fled France during religious persecutions. Whatever their varying personal fortunes might be, these men were never full-fledged members of the establishment.

[127] Ibid., x, 278.
[128] Mill, *Principles*, Ashley edn., pp. 211–217; Toronto edn., pp. 210–214.
[129] Rae, *Life of Adam Smith*, pp. 26–29.
[130] Ibid., pp. 26, 208.

CHAPTER II

Macroeconomics

CLASSICAL ECONOMICS was much more than a miscellaneous collection of theories and doctrines. Its particular theories and policy prescriptions revolved around a single central concern: economic growth. Unlike modern growth theory, classical economists were not primarily concerned with the adjustments of the economy to the growth process, but with how such a process could be generated and sustained. The full title of Adam Smith's classic included the nature and *causes* of the wealth of nations.[1] Even the static Ricardian model was concerned, as a practical matter, with the progress of the economy toward the stationary state, and with what this implied for the functional distribution of income "in different stages of society."[2] The static concept of Say's Law became so entangled in growth theory as to confuse the issues involved in the "general glut" controversy and to cause that controversy to continue needlessly for years. Even such verbal disputes as that revolving around the difference between "productive" and "unproductive" labor (or consumption) turned on growth problems—

[1] Adam Smith, *An Inquiry into the Nature and Causes of the Wealth of Nations* (New York: Modern Library, 1937).

[2] David Ricardo, *The Works and Correspondence of David Ricardo*, ed. Piero Sraffa (Cambridge: Cambridge University Press, 1951-55), I, 5.

in this case, the growth-promoting ("productive") labor, spending, or consumption being distinguished from the non-growth-promoting ("unproductive") counterpart by the indirect criterion of product materiality rather than the direct criterion of accumulability. Classical microeconomics revolved as much around economic growth as did classical macroeconomics. Ricardian rent theory and Malthusian population theory, though based on behavior in specific markets (agriculture and labor), dealt with the growth of the economy as a whole.

This concern for promoting growth had a very serious practical basis. Smith argued that it was not in the wealthiest, but in the fastest growing, countries that wages were highest.[3] Only the maintenance of growth kept wages above the subsistence level.

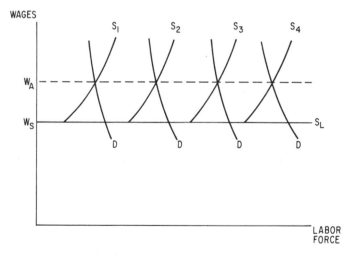

FIGURE I

[3] Smith, *Wealth of Nations*, p. 59.

34

The whole classical school—including some who were heretical on other points—accepted the proposition that the long-run supply curve (S_L) of labor was infinitely elastic at some conventional subsistence level. The short-run supply curves (S_1, S_2, S_3, S_4), were rising, since additional labor could be obtained from a given population only by offering higher wages to get more hours from existing workers and/or attract entry into the labor force. Therefore, an ever-increasing demand for labor (D_1, D_2, D_3, D_4) was needed to keep the actual wages (W_A) above the subsistence wages (W_s). If the "stationary state" of Ricardo were ever reached in reality, wages would fall to subsistence. Therefore the maintenance of the on-growing growth process was essential for the well-being of the bulk of society. The same preoccupation dominated the dissenters from the classical tradition as well as the classical economists themselves.

SAY'S LAW

There has been considerable controversy as to whether Say's Law was in fact the product of J. B. Say or of James Mill. Substantial elements of it had, in fact, appeared earlier in *The Wealth of Nations* (1776). A still earlier version—in some ways better rounded than that of the classical period—existed in *L'Ordre naturel* (1767) by the physiocrat, Mercier de la Rivière, whose writings were known to Say, Mill, and Adam Smith.[4]

Mercier de la Rivière stated that all buyers must be sellers and all sellers must be buyers, that the respective

[4] Jean-Baptiste Say, *A Treatise on Political Economy*, trans. by Clement C. Biddle (Philadelphia: Grigg & Elliott, 1834), p. xxxvii; James Mill, *Commerce Defended* (London: C. & R. Baldwin, 1808), p. 76n; Smith, *Wealth of Nations*, p. 643.

"sums of these two operations must be equal to each other," and that sales "even in money" were "only exchanges of equal values."[5] This *ex post* identity was only one facet of the argument in *L'Ordre naturel*, as in later classical economics. Money was "only a *means of exchange*" not to be confused with "true wealth."[6] Money was an "intermediary standard,"[7] and a distraction which "only threw ideas into such confusion" that the basic barter was overlooked.[8] Although the equality of supply and demand was sometimes expressed as an *ex post* identity of purchases and sales, it was essentially a behavioral theory of an *ex ante* equality of supply and demand. One must be a seller in order to be a buyer,[9] for sales which one "proposes to make" can continually take place only insofar as one has spent the proceeds of other sales, the various transactions "alternately" providing each other with markets.[10] The correct proportions between supply and demand "will be established by themselves" through the workings of the market, since it is "impossible" that changes in demand and supply will not bring on changes of value which reestablish equilibrium.[11] According to Mercier de la Rivière, "equilibrium can only be deranged accidently";[12] it will "maintain itself always and *necessarily*, provided that we do nothing to disturb it."[13]

The equality of supply and demand, or of the opposite flows of goods and money, did not mean for Mercier de

[5] Pierre Francois Joachim Henri Le Mercier de la Rivière, *L'Ordre naturel et essentiel des sociétés politiques* (London: Jean Nourse, 1767), II, 249.

[6] Ibid., p. 337.

[8] Ibid., p. 262.

[10] Ibid., p. 258.

[12] Ibid., p. 291.

[7] Ibid., pp. 262–264.

[9] Ibid., p. 264.

[11] Ibid., p. 296.

[13] Ibid., p. 140.

la Rivière that aggregate output could not change. "Consumption"—which meant aggregate demand as a whole (including investment), in the physiocrats as in the classical economists—"has no known limits,"[14] but at any given time it may be insufficient to cause the total current output to be reproduced. Consumption was the measure of *reproduction* (Y_{t+1}),[15] for "production which remains unconsumed" would "degenerate" in utility and value and "subsequently advances would cease to be made" for their production.[16] By "consumed" was not meant merely that the market was cleared, for consumption meant demand *at cost-covering prices*:[17]

When we say that consumption is the proportional measure of reproduction, it must be understood to mean a consumption which returns a profit to those whose labor and expenses will reproduce the output; a consumption which was of no use to them would certainly not cause them to labor and to spend in order to renew the things which were absorbed.[18]

J. B. Say was openly contemptuous of Mercier de la Rivière's "tiresome trash,"[19] despite (or because of?) his clear anticipation of Say's Law. By interpreting consumption in the narrow sense of consumer goods and by reading the classical emphasis on growth into this argument, Say and Mill were able to represent *L'Ordre naturel* as claiming that spending for consumer goods promoted growth more than spending for investment goods.[20] Later

[14] Ibid., p. 272.   [15] Ibid., pp. 138, 142, 250.
[16] Ibid., p. 250.   [17] Ibid., pp. 138, 271.
[18] Ibid., pp. 138–139.
[19] Say, *A Treatise on Political Economy*, p. xxxvii.
[20] Jean-Baptiste Say, *Traité d'économie politique* (Paris: Deg-

interpreters have made the physiocrats predecessors of such economic dissenters as Sismondi and Malthus (and, ultimately, Keynes),[21] but they were equally predecessors of classical orthodoxy.[22] Looked at another way, the physiocrats made Say's Law and equilibrium income theory mutually compatible, as they were *not* to be regarded for most of the next 200 years.

Adam Smith separated aggregate demand into investment and consumer goods components. He argued that savings or "parsimony" was "the immediate cause of the increase of capital," and conversely the increase of capital was the inevitable effect of savings: "What is annually saved is as regularly consumed as what is annually spent, and nearly in the same time too."[23] Money "will not be allowed to lie idle."[24] There is only a transactions demand for money. It "can serve no other purpose besides purchasing goods," and it is desired "not for its own sake" but for the sake of what people can purchase with it.[25] Therefore, "though a particular merchant, with an abundance of goods in his warehouse, may sometimes be

---

erville, 1803), ii, 358–359; James Mill, *Commerce Defended*, p. 76n.

[21] Joseph J. Spengler, "The Physiocrats and Say's Law of Markets," *Essays in Economic Thought*, ed. J. J. Spengler and W. R. Allen (Chicago: Rand McNally & Co. 1960), pp. 161–214; Ronald L. Meek, *The Economics of Physiocracy* (Cambridge: Harvard University Press, 1963).

[22] J. B. Say's mentor, DuPont deNemours, reminded Say how much of the latter's own analysis derived from the Physiocrats. Jean-Baptiste Say, *Œuvres Diverses de J.-B. Say* (Paris: Guillauminet et Cie, 1848), p. 365.

[23] Smith, *Wealth of Nations*, p. 321.

[24] Ibid., p. 323.   [25] Ibid., p. 407.

ruined by not being able to sell them in time, a nation or country is not liable to the same accident."[26] Though here was the essence of Say's Law, Smith did not have the dogmatism of some later classical writers. His doctrines on money were true "in the long-run" and he acknowledged that "goods do not always draw money so readily as money draws goods," that money "is not always obtainable with equal readiness" for goods.[27] But there was no elaboration of such qualifying statements or their implications.

Say's Law, as it emerged during the classical period, was a cluster of related propositions contributed and refined by a number of individuals. Some of these propositions were fully accepted by the dissenting economists of the "general glut" school and some were partially or completely rejected by them. Some have come down through history and others have quietly disappeared along the way. A present-day analysis of Say's Law and of the controversies revolving around it cannot proceed as if the earlier economists were necessarily arguing about the modern doctrine that carries the same name. Say's Law in classical economics involved six major propositions:

1. The total factor payments received for producing a given volume (or value) of output are necessarily sufficient to purchase that volume (or value) of output.[28]
2. There is no loss of purchasing power anywhere in the economy, for people save only to the

---

[26] Loc. cit.   [27] Loc. cit.
[28] James Mill, *Commerce Defended*, p. 81.

extent of their desire to invest and do not hold money beyond their transactions needs during the current period.[29]

3. Investment is only an internal transfer, not a net reduction, of aggregate demand.[30] The same amount that could have been spent by the thrifty consumer will be spent by the capitalists and/or the workers in the investment goods sector.[31]

4. In real terms, supply equals demand *ex ante*, since each individual produces only because of, and to the extent of, his demand for other goods.[32] (Sometimes this doctrine was supported by demonstrating that supply equals demand *ex post*.)[33]

5. A higher rate of savings will cause a higher rate of subsequent growth in aggregate output.[34]

[29] Ibid., p. 83; Smith, *Wealth of Nations*, pp. 321–322.

[30] Smith, *Wealth of Nations*, p. 322; Say, *Traité d'économie politique*, 1803 edn. II, 177n.

[31] John Stuart Mill, *Principles of Political Economy*, Toronto edn., p. 573.

[32] James Mill, *Elements of Political Economy*, 3rd edn. (London: Henry G. Bohn, 1844), pp. 228, 231, 237, 241; John Stuart Mill, *Principles*, Toronto edn., pp. 572–573; John Stuart Mill, *Collected Works*, Vol. IV: *Essays on Economics and Society*, 17–18, 42.

[33] James Mill argued that "annual purchases and sales" will "always balance" in his *Commerce Defended*, p. 82; J. R. McCulloch declared that there cannot "be any *selling* without an equal *buying*" (*Edinburgh Review*, March 1821, p. 108); Robert Torrens regarded supply and demand as "convertible" terms (*Edinburgh Review*, October 1819, p. 470.

[34] Smith, *Wealth of Nations*, p. 322; [James Mill], "Lord Lauderdale on Public Wealth," *The Literary Journal*, July 1804, p. 12; James Mill, *Commerce Defended*, pp. 70, 71, 74, 78.

6. Disequilibrium in the economy can exist only because the internal proportions of output differ from consumers' preferred mix—*not* because output is excessive in the aggregate.[35]

The first three propositions were never in dispute among any of the recognized economists of the classical period, orthodox or dissenting. These propositions served to refute popular fears that the rapidly growing output and sharp depressions of that period implied that some absolute limit to economic growth had been reached. The general glut economists were as zealous in refuting these popular notions as were the supporters of Say's Law.[36] With the exception of Malthus, they were also

[35] Say, *Traité d'économie politique*, 1803 edn., II, 178; Ricardo, *Works*, VIII, 277; ibid., II, 306; Robert Torrens, *An Essay on the Production of Wealth* (London: Longman, Hurst, Rees, Orme, and Brown, 1821), pp. 391, 392, 396; John Ramsey McCulloch, *Principles of Political Economy*, 5th edn. (Edinburgh: Adam and Charles Black, 1864), p. 145; James Mill, *Commerce Defended*, p. 85; James Mill, *Elements of Political Economy*, pp. 234–235, 240, 241; Harriet Martineau, *The Moral of Many Fables* (London: Charles Fox, 1834), p. 128.

[36] According to Malthus, the secular growth of the economy "is absolutely unlimited" (letter in Ricardo, *Works*, VI, 318). Despite his attack on Say's Law, "the question of a glut is exclusively whether it may be general as well as particular and not whether it may be permanent as well as temporary." T. R. Malthus, *Definitions in Political Economy* (London: John Murray, 1827), p. 62. Sismondi likewise had a theory of short-run aggregate disequilibrium, but denied secular stagnation. According to Sismondi, the "natural path of nations" is "the progressive increase of their prosperity, the increase and consequence of their demand for new products and of the means of paying for them." J.C.L. Simonde de Sismondi, *Nouveaux Principes d'économie politique*, 3rd edn. (Geneva-Paris: Edition Jeheber, 1953),

as zealous as the orthodox economists in emphasizing the "real" variables in the economy and treating money as only a "veil" which obscured the workings of the economy without affecting end-results.[37]

The last three propositions were the focus of controversy. The fundamental disagreement was over the classical denial of an equilibrium aggregate output (number 6). Sismondi developed a theory of aggregate output equilibrium determined by a balancing of the declining utility of additional output and of the rising disutility of labor. This was analyzed on the individual level through Robinson Crusoe models,[38] and extended to the economy by analogy[39]—with the important note that the complexities of a modern economy made individual miscalculations inevitable, and therefore an aggregate balance problematical.[40] A very similar theory of equilibrium income reappeared in Malthus' *Principles* a year after Sismondi's *Nouveaux Principes*, though developed by Malthus directly on the economy level and emphasizing the possibilities of a mistaken, excessive volume of savings. According to Malthus, a transitory increment of savings and investment may fail to yield an "adequate" return

---

II, 308. Similar ideas are found in other critics of Say's Law. See James Maitland, 8th Earl of Lauderdale, *An Inquiry into the Nature and Origin of Public Wealth* (New York: Augustus M. Kelley, 1962 [originally 1804], p. 229; Thomas Chalmers, *On Political Economy* (Glasgow: William Collins, 1832), pp. 96, 158.

[37] Sismondi, *Nouveaux Principes*, I, 118; Lauderdale, *Nature and Origin of Public Wealth*, pp. 3-4, 212; Chalmers, *On Political Economy*, p. 158.

[38] Sismondi, *Nouveaux Principes*, I, 71-75.

[39] Ibid., p. 110. [40] Ibid., pp. 250-251.

to investors, so that there is "first an unnatural demand for labour, and then a necessary and sudden diminution of such demand" as disappointed investors disinvest, so as to "throw the rising generation out of employment."[41]

With Say and especially the Ricardians, Say's Law took on the meaning that there was no such thing as an equilibrium level of aggregate output. The classical economists were never guilty of the absurdity of denying the existence of depressions, unemployment, or unsold goods, as sometimes claimed in the literature.[42] They recognized such phenomena as effects of production that was internally out of proportion as far as product mix was concerned, but *not* excessive in the aggregate. In John Stuart Mill's words, "production is not excessive, but merely ill-assorted."[43] To Ricardo "it is at all times the bad adaptation of the commodities produced to the wants of mankind which is the specific evil, and not the abundance of commodities."[44] "Men err in their productions," he said, "there is no deficiency of demand."[45] Lesser lights pushed this doctrine to its logical conclusion: equilibrium could be restored by increasing the output of those products undersupplied relative to others—that is by an increase of aggregate output. According to McCulloch, a glut of the market was "not a consequence of production being too much increased, but of its being too little increased." The remedy: "Increase it more."[46] Sismondi ac-

---

[41] Ricardo, *Works*, IX, 20.
[42] Robert L. Heilbroner, *The Worldly Philosophers*, 3rd edn. (New York: Simon & Schuster, 1967), p. 91.
[43] J. S. Mill, *Principles*, Toronto edn., p. 573; Ashley edn., p. 559.
[44] Ricardo, *Works*, II, 306.   [45] Ibid., VIII, 277.
[46] *Edinburgh Review*, March 1821, pp. 106–107.

curately summed up the differences between the supporters of Say's Law and the proponents of equilibrium income or "general glut" theories when he said:

You have produced too much, say some; you have not produced enough, say the others. Equilibrium will be reestablished, say the first, peace and prosperity will return again only when you have consumed all the surplus of commodities which remain unsold in the market and when you regulate your future production by the demand of the buyer. Equilibrium will return again, say the others, provided that you redouble your efforts to invest as well as to produce. You are deceived when you believe our markets are overstocked. Only half our stores are filled. Let us fill the other half, and these new riches, by being exchanged for the others, will revive commerce.[47]

The issue—whether aggregate supply always equals aggregate demand—turned on ambiguities in the concept of "demand" as well as in the concept of "cost" underlying supply. For the Ricardians, "demand" was simply the quantity demanded.[48] For Sismondi and Malthus, "demand" meant the quantity demanded at cost-covering prices, where "cost" was the *ex ante* supply price, not simply the *ex post* factor payments, "not what it has cost now, but what it would cost hereafter."[49] Differences between expectations *ex ante* and results *ex post* permitted aggregate supply to differ from aggregate demand, even with no leakages from the circular flow. None of the

[47] Sismondi, *Nouveaux Principes*, II, 253.
[48] Ricardo, *Works*, I, 382–383; ibid., VI, 109.
[49] J.C.L. Simonde de Sismondi, *Études sur l'économie politique* (Paris: Treuttel et Wurtz, 1837–1838), II, 381.

major general glut theorists—Sismondi, Malthus, Lauderdale, or Chalmers—based his theory on leakages from the circular flow, and all except Malthus went to considerable pains to disassociate themselves from those who did.[50] Malthus felt that too much attention had already been devoted to correcting "the absurd notions of the mercantile classes."[51]

In contrast to Ricardian comparative statics, the proponents of equilibrium income or general glut theories reasoned in dynamic terms. Sismondi originated period analysis in his *Richesse Commerciale* in 1803, where arithmetic examples and algebraic equations showed a model in which the output of one year was 2.5 times the wages fund of the previous year, in countries with various kinds of international trade balances.[52] Malthus' verbal models were equally dynamic, though not so clearly period analysis. The Ricardian refutation of the doctrine that some levels of aggregate output could be above the equilibrium—a "general glut"—relied heavily on comparative statics. They showed that "after the readjustment has been affected,"[53] "after the lapse of such a period as would permit . . . transfer to new businesses,"[54] "after an unconsiderable interval,"[55] there can be no "lasting"[56] or "permanent"[57] glut, for people will not

[50] See n. 37 and sec. II of the text.
[51] Ricardo, *Works*, VI, 21.
[52] J.C.L. Simonde [de Sismondi], *De la Richess Commerciale* (Geneva. J. J. Paschoud, 1803), I, 99–108.
[53] Torrens, *Edinburgh Review*, October 1819, p. 473.
[54] McCulloch, *Principles of Political Economy*, 5th edn., p. 149.
[55] Ricardo, *Works*, II, 390.
[56] McCulloch, *Principles of Political Economy*, p. 144.
[57] Ibid., p. 145; J. S. Mill, *Principles*, Ashley edn., p. 561; Toronto edn., p. 575.

"continue" to produce unprofitably,[58] and the situation will be automatically "rectified"[59] and "infallibly produce its own remedy."[60]

Such statements brought fierce denunciations from contemporaries that it was "quite useless to repeat, like a parrot, that things have a tendency to find their own level,"[61] and that "this tendency, in the natural course of things, to cure a glut or scarcity, is no more a proof that such evils have never existed, than the tendency of the healing processes of nature to cure some disorders without assistance from man, is a proof that such disorders have not existed."[62] Modern interpreters have overlooked the blind persistence with which the Ricardians translated others' dynamic analyses into comparative statics terms, and have assumed that the general glut controversy was a controversy over permanent secular stagnation[63] rather than cyclical fluctuations and over the concept of an equilibrium income. As Malthus said, "the question of a glut is exclusively whether it may be general, as well as

[58] J. S. Mill, *Collected Works*, IV, 17.

[59] McCulloch, *Principles of Political Economy*, p. 145.

[60] James Mill, *Elements of Political Economy*, p. 242.

[61] [Samuel Bailey], *An Inquiry into Those Principles Respecting the Nature of Demand and the Necessity of Consumption Lately Advocated by Mr. Malthus* (London: R. Hunter, 1821). Bailey's authorship of this anonymous pamphlet is indicated in my "Samuel Bailey Revisited," *Economica*, November 1970, pp. 402–408.

[62] Malthus, *Definitions in Political Economy*, pp. 62–63.

[63] See, for example, Don Patinkin, *Money, Interest and Prices*, 2nd edn. (New York: Harper & Row, 1965), p. 364; Mark Blaug, *Economic Theory in Retrospect* (Homewood: Richard D. Irwin, 1962), p. 140: Mark Blaug, *Ricardian Economics* (New Haven: Yale University Press, 1958), p. 93.

particular, and not whether it may be permanent as well as temporary."[64]

Eventually Ricardo grudgingly yielded somewhat to Malthus' ideas in the dynamic sense that was so alien to his approach.[65] The real conversion was that of Jean-Baptiste Say himself. In the fifth edition of his *Traité d'économie politique* (1826) he openly disavowed the doctrine that there were no short-run limits to production, and in his correspondence of this period he repudiated the Ricardians and their "syllogisms," "obscure metaphysics," "abstract principles," and "vain subtleties." He admitted to Malthus that Say's Law was "subject to some restrictions"[66] and to Sismondi that the fifth edition of his *Traité* contained a "concession" to the latter's theory of equilibrium income.[67] In the *Traité* itself, Say now observed that "it is only with abstract quantities that there are infinite progressions" while "we are studying practical political economy here."[68] He then argued in Sismondian fashion:

> Beyond a certain point, the difficulties which accompany production, and which are in general overcome by productive services, grow at an increasing rate and soon surpass the satisfaction which can result from the use made of the product. Thenceforth a useful thing may certainly be created, but its utility will not be worth what it cost, and it will not fulfill the essential

[64] Malthus, *Definitions in Political Economy*, p. 62.

[65] Ricardo, *Works*, IX, 15, 131.

[66] J. B. Say, *Œuvres diverses*, p. 505.

[67] See J.C.L. Simonde de Sismondi, *Political Economy and the Philosophy of Government* (London: John Chapman, 1847), p. 449.

[68] Say, *Traité d'économie politique*, 5th edn., I, 194–195.

condition of a product, which is to at least equal in value its costs of production.[69]

Say's later textbook *Cours complet d'économie politique* (1828–29), followed the chapter on Say's Law with a chapter on "the limits of production,"[70] which repeated the same general reasoning.[71] Unfortunately, neither this work nor that part of his correspondence has ever been translated into English, nor has the fifth edition of his *Traité*. Moreover, Say's "recantation" on this point made no visible impression on the British classical school.

John Stuart Mill's role in the development of Say's Law was an unusual one. On the one hand, his *Principles of Political Economy* (1848) repeated the same arguments and misinterpretations that had existed at the outset of the general glut controversy, nearly 30 years earlier. Throughout Mill's writings, Sismondi, Malthus, and their allies were depicted as believers in secular stagnation;[72] their dynamic analysis was answered in comparative statics terms[73] and supply was said to equal demand "by the metaphysical necessity of the case,"[74] pos-

---

[69] Ibid., p. 195.

[70] Say, *Cours complet d'économie politique*, I, 345.

[71] ". . . products in general can be multiplied and purchased by one another until a limit which no one knows precisely how to determine, and which depends on the local circumstances of each country; beyond that limit, certain products become too expensive for the utility which they have to indemnify their consumers for what is required to obtain them." Ibid., pp. 346–347.

[72] J. S. Mill, *Principles*, Toronto edn., pp. 570–571, 575, 576; *Collected Works*, IV, 16–17.

[73] Ibid., *Principles*, Toronto, edn., pp. 570–571; ibid., *Collected Works*, IV, 16–17.

[74] J. S. Mill, *Essays on Some Unsettled Questions of Political Economy* (London: John W. Parker, 1844), p. 69.

sessing "all the certainty of a mathematical demonstration" because it depended upon "the very meaning of the words, demand and supply"[75] rather than being contingent on the validity of a particular theory of behavior. On the other hand, once having disposed of the heretics and their supposed doctrine, Mill discussed the real substance of the issue more clearly and thoroughly than any other classical economist. Mill was, in fact, the first of the classical economists to explore directly the possibility of a demand for money beyond the transactions demand. In his *Essays on Some Unsettled Questions of Political Economy*, he said:

> Although he who sells, really sells only to buy, he needs not buy at the same moment when he sells; and he does not therefore necessarily add to the *immediate* demand for one commodity when he adds to the supply of another. The buying and selling being now separated, it may very well occur, that there may be, at some given time, a very general inclination to sell with as little delay as possible, accompanied with an equally general inclination to defer all purchases as long as possible.[76]

He was still more explicit in his *Principles*: "I have already described the state of the markets for commodities which accompanies what is termed a commercial crisis. At such times there is really an excess of all commodities above the money demand: in other words, there is an under supply of money."[77]

[75] J. S. Mill, *Collected Works*, IV, 16.
[76] J. S. Mill, *Essays on Some Unsettled Questions of Political Economy*, p. 70.
[77] J. S. Mill, *Principles*, Toronto edn., p. 574.

Ad hoc suggestions of deficient money demand had been made by Say and Torrens, and implied by Adam Smith, and a deficiency of demand had been dubbed synonymous with excess output by G. P. Scrope.[78] Mill also set forth a theory of oversaving very similar to that of Malthus, Lauderdale, and Chalmers:

> ... unless a considerable portion of the annual increase of capital were either periodically destroyed, or exported for foreign investment, the country would speedily attain to the point at which further accumulation would cease, or at least spontaneously slacken, so as no longer to overpass the march of invention in the arts which produce the necessaries of life. In such a state of things as this, a sudden addition to the capital of the country, unaccompanied by any increase of productive power, would be of but transitory duration; since, by depressing profits and interest, it would either diminish by a corresponding amount the savings which would be made from income in the year or two following, or it would cause an equivalent amount to be sent abroad, or to be wasted in rash speculations.[79]

The doctrine that savings promote growth was a prime target of the dissenters, from Lauderdale in 1804 through Chalmers in 1832. All dealt with the dynamic effects of a transitory increment of savings beyond what would be

[78] Jean-Baptiste Say, *Letters to Thomas Robert Malthus* (London: George Hardings Bookshop, Ltd., 1936 [originally London, 1821]), pp. 45n–46n; Torrens, *An Essay on the Production of Wealth*, pp. 421–422; Smith, *Wealth of Nations*, p. 407; George Poulett Scrope; *Principles of Political Economy* (London: Longman, Rees, Orme, Brown, Green & Longman, 1833), pp. 214–215.

[79] J. S. Mill, *Principles*, Toronto edn., p. 747.

forthcoming at the *ex post* rate of return. All recognized that technological improvements tend to increase the equilibrium volume of profitable investment over time, but argued that at any *given* time, under given conditions of technology and taste, there was a limit to sustainable investment.[80] Sismondi summed up this viewpoint when he said that "a nation which cannot make progress should not make savings."[81]

The classical rejoinders either (1) implicitly assumed that "savings" meant equilibrium increments of savings or (2) pointed out the transience of the situation created. Not all the classical economists followed Adam Smith in promoting savings as a growth-producing factor. Ricardo disavowed any intention to advocate growth promoting policies in general,[82] though Say and James Mill were such advocates.[83] Much of the general glut controversy revolved around this now-discarded growth feature of Say's Law. Neither side claimed that saving and investment would remain in disequilibrium in an unregulated market, but the general glut theorists assumed that government fiscal activities sometimes artificially increased savings and investment beyond a sustainable level.[84] They

[80] Lauderdale, *Nature and Origin of Public Wealth*, pp. 227–228; Sismondi, *Nouveaux Principes*, I, 247–248. This is more implicit in T. R. Malthus, *Principles of Political Economy*, 2nd edn. (New York: Augustus M. Kelley, 1951 [originally 1836]), pp. 328, 351–352; Chalmers, *On Political Economy*, p. 136.

[81] Sismondi, *Nouveaux Principes*, I, 248.

[82] Ricardo, *Works*, II, 338.

[83] Say, *A Treatise on Political Economy*, p. 143; James Mill, *Commerce Defended*, p. 88.

[84] The Earl of Lauderdale, *Three Letters to the Duke of Wellington* (London: John Murray, 1829), p. 134; Sismondi, *Nouveaux Principes*, I, 328–329; ibid., II, 193, 308.

were not discussing "voluntary parsimony," as James Mill noted,[85] so this aspect of the controversy had little in common with modern post-Keynesian controversy, other than the use of similar words.

The doctrine that supply equals demand *ex ante* was sometimes supported by showing that supply equals demand *ex post*. McCulloch pointed out that there cannot "be any *selling* without an equal *buying*."[86] Torrens said that supply and demand were "correlative and convertible" terms while James Mill said that "annual purchases and sales" will "always balance."[87] John Stuart Mill and J. B. Say also had tautological versions.[88] This is not to claim that the whole argument was purely tautological. It was simply defended this way on occasion under polemical stress.

MONETARY THEORY

Several factors add to the difficulty of understanding classical monetary theory or present plausible bases for misinterpretations:

1. The anti-mercantilist origins of classical economics were a continuing verbal influence producing sweeping statements about the unimportance of

[85] [James Mill], "Lord Lauderdale on Public Wealth," p. 14.
[86] *Edinburgh Review*, March 1821, p. 108.
[87] James Mill, *Commerce Defended*, p. 82.
[88] [J. S. Mill], "War Expenditure," *Westminster Review*, July 1824, p. 41; J. S. Mill, *Essays on Some Unsettled Questions of Political Economy*, p. 69. To Say the very definition of "production" or of "product" included sale at cost-covering prices: Say, *Traité d'économie politique*, 5th edn., p. 195; Say, *Cours complet d'économie politique*, 1, 345–346; Say, *Œuvres diverses*, p. 513.

money—even in the midst of explanations of its effects on real variables.

2. Ricardian comparative statics and concentration on long-run equilibrium assumed away many transitional monetary phenomena, especially in Ricardo's *Principles*—though his polemical pamphlets and correspondence dealt with such problems, even if sometimes somewhat grudgingly.

3. The tendency of the classical economists—and their contemporary opponents—to conceive of causation in sequential terms (rather than in terms of reciprocal interaction or mutual determination)[89] meant that money was sometimes treated as causally neutral when a given series of events was considered to *originate* with a change in some real variable, even though the resulting monetary phenomena were important features of the adjustment process.

4. Keynes' well-known polemical interpretations of classical monetary theory make it difficult to read classical statements with fresh eyes or in the context in which they were originally made.

[89] Ricardo's preoccupation with an "invariable measure of value" was an attempt to analyze a change in the relative value of goods in such a way as to discover which one had "really" changed—that is where the change had *originated* in some change of production cost (Ricardo, *Works*, I, 17 18). Malthus approached monetary theory in the same way: money supply changes were not an "original cause" or the "mainspring" of the real phenomena (*Edinburgh Review*, February 1811, pp. 359, 343), though they might be part of the "necessary consequences" of changes in real variables (*Definitions in Political Economy*, p. 66).

Many classical monetary doctrines can be traced to *The Wealth of Nations*, whose consuming purpose of refuting mercantilism caused many statements to be made within the framework of a mercantilism-versus-laissez-faire controversy which could not stand alone outside such a framework. Apparently these statements were not meant to stand alone outside such a framework, for other statements were made apparently contradicting them. As already noted,[90] the mercantilists tended to conceive of wealth as a stock of money or gold, rather than as a flow of real goods and services. Smith and the classical school not only denied that money was wealth[91] or capital[92] but asserted that money was wanted solely for transactions needs—"money can serve no other purpose besides purchasing goods"[93]—and that it did not affect such real variables as the rate of interest,[94] which depended upon the return on real capital.[95] The recipient of money wants it "only for the purpose of employing that money again immediately"[96] in some other transaction, for purchasing

[90] Chapter 1 above.

[91] Smith, *Wealth of Nations*, pp. 398–399; Ricardo, *Works*, III, p. 145; J. S. Mill, *Principles*, Toronto edn., pp. 4–5, 7, 71–72, 505, 592.

[92] Smith, *Wealth of Nations*, pp. 334, 335; Ricardo, *Works*, III, 273, 286; J. S. Mill, *Principles*, Toronto edn., p. 508.

[93] Smith, *Wealth of Nations*, p. 407.

[94] Smith, *Wealth of Nations*, p. 337; Ricardo, *Works*, I, 363–364; ibid., III, 25–26, 89, 90, 91, 92, 137, 143, 150, 341, 374–375, 376; J. S. Mill, *Principles*, Toronto edn., p. 655; ibid., *Collected Works*, IV, 98.

[95] Smith, *Wealth of Nations*, pp. 336, 339; Ricardo, *Works*, I, 363; ibid., III, 25–26, 143, 150, 374–375, ibid., VI, 94–95, 103, 104, 108, 110; ibid., VII, 197; J. S. Mill, *Collected Works*, IV, 102, 300–302.

[96] J. B. Say "Catechism of Political Economy," reprinted in

"forthwith"[97] something else, according to Say and his followers.[98]

The opponents of Say's Law were no less zealous in promoting the same monetary doctrines. According to Sismondi, money is "immediately" respent,[99] for to allow "useless stagnation" of money would mean "lost interest."[100] Whether money income is consumed or saved, "it is equally spent in either way,"[101] according to Chalmers, so that there was no change in aggregate demand. Sismondi, Chalmers, and Lauderdale deliberately developed their economic analysis "without speaking of money,"[102] without the complications of "overgrown financial arrangements,"[103] for money was "not necessary" to the real phenomena in question, and served only to "obscure the character of the proceeding without essentially changing it."[104] Money was only a "veil," to the general glut theorists as well as to the supporters of Say's Law. The lone apparent exception to this was Malthus, who *mentioned* money as a neglected element,[105] but who

Kelley edition of *Letters to Mr. Malthus* (New York: Augustus M. Kelley, 1967), p. 104.

[97] Say, *A Treatise on Political Economy*, p. 138.

[98] McCulloch, *Principles of Political Economy*, 5th edn., p. 157.

[99] Sismondi, *Nouveaux Principes*, I, 278; idem., *Political Economy*, p. 79.

[100] Sismondi, *Nouveaux Principes*, II, 2; see also Sismondi, *Richesse Commerciale*, I, 33n.

[101] Chalmers, *On Political Economy*, p. 16.

[102] Sismondi, *Nouveaux Principes*, I, 118.

[103] Lauderdale, *Nature and Origin of Public Wealth*, p. 212.

[104] Chalmers, *On Political Economy*, p. 158.

[105] Malthus, *Principles of Political Economy*, 2nd edn., p 1324n; Malthus, *Definitions in Political Economy*, pp. 54, 60n.

did not explore monetary phenomena or incorporate it into his analysis any more than the others.

What is significant is whether either group meant this in the unqualified way in which it was sometimes expressed. For the same Adam Smith who asserted that "money can serve no other purpose besides purchasing goods," said on the same page that "goods do not always draw money so readily as money draws goods," though "in the long-run" they attract each other. The same J. B. Say who referred to "immediate" respending also referred to idle balances accumulating beyond transactions needs during a depression; the same Sismondi who asserted that money was "immediately" respent, also traced the effects of credit contraction in a crisis.[106] Chalmers even referred to capitalists' demand for money wealth as such, aside from any transactions which might be contemplated.[107]

Part of the apparent ambivalence of classical economics in monetary theory was due to implicit shifts between long-run and short-run perspectives, and in part to shifts between arguments against mercantilism (and/or its popular remnants) and general analyses of monetary phenomena. The effect of the money supply on the interest rate illustrates both kinds of shifts. Hume, Smith, Ricardo, and J. S. Mill all denied that the quantity of money effected the interest rate[108]—in the comparative

[106] Smith, *Wealth of Nations*, p. 407; Say, *Letters to Thomas Robert Malthus*, pp. 45n–46n; Sismondi, *Nouveaux Principes*, II, 83, 84.

[107] Chalmers, *On Political Economy*, pp. 184–185.

[108] David Hume, "Of Interest," *Writings on Economics*, ed. Eugene Rotwein (Madison: University of Wisconsin Press, 1970), pp. 47, 51, 56, 57; Smith, *Wealth of Nations*, p. 337;

56

statics sense that once a given amount of money (or gold) had been absorbed into the economy and prices had adjusted accordingly, there was no reason to expect the final equilibrium interest rate to be any different from what it had been initially. They stated that during the transition period, however, the interest rate would tend to be lowered,[109] idle resources activated,[110] and real wealth increased.[111] Conversely, if there is a contraction of money or credit, then during the transition, there may be "the most disastrous consequences"[112] domestically as well as disturbances in the equilibrium of imports and exports.[113] A strong *precautionary* demand for money may develop,[114] raising the rate of interest.[115] The rate of interest is affected in the short run by changes in the demand for money,[116] as well as by changes in the supply of money.[117]

Ricardo, *Works*, ı, 363-364; ibid., ııı, 25-26, 89, 90, 91, 92, 137, 143, 150, 341, 374-375, 376; J. S. Mill, *Collected Works*, ıv, 98.

[109] Hume, *Writings on Economics*, p. 57, Ricardo, *Works*, ı, 297-298; J. S. Mill, *Collected Works*, ıv, 97; ibid., *Principles*, Toronto edn., pp. 655-656, 657, 678n, 679n.

[110] J. S. Mill, *Collected Works*, ıv, 189, 190, 197; Henry Thornton, *An Enquiry into the Nature and Effects of the Paper Credit of Great Britain*, ed. F. A. v. Hayek (New York: Augustus M. Kelley, 1965), pp. 236, 237, 238, 239, 250.

[111] Hume, *Writings on Economics*, pp. 37, 38, 40, 91-92, 93-94; Smith, *Wealth of Nations*, p. 304; J. S. Mill, *Principles*, Toronto edn., pp. 565-566.

[112] Ricardo, *Works*, ııı, 94.   [113] Ibid., p. 245.

[114] J. S. Mill, *Principles*, Toronto edn., p. 654; ibid., ıv, 671.

[115] Ibid., *Principles*, Toronto edn., p. 654.

[116] Ibid., pp. 654, 678n.

[117] Hume, *Writings on Economics*, p. 57; J. S. Mill, *Principles*, Toronto edn., pp. 655-656; ibid., *Collected Works*, ıv, 97.

The leading monetary work of the classical period, Henry Thornton's *Paper Credit of Great Britain* (1802) carefully noted the "immediate" and "temporary" reactions to monetary changes,[118] pointing out that adjustments are "certainly not instantaneous,"[119] and that money may be "hoarded" during a period of "alarm."[120] He also noted "the fresh industry which is excited" during an increase of the money supply.[121] It distinguished these dynamic changes from the effects to be expected after a changed quantity of money "shall have been for some time stationary" and producing its "full effect." In this long-run equilibrium sense, the interest rate is unaffected by the quantity of money,[122] for in the long run it is only a "progressive augmentation" of money "and not the magnitude of its existing amount" which can lower interest rates.[123]

Thornton's careful separation of short-run transitional effects from long-run equilibrium effects contrasts sharply with Ricardo's repeated interpretation of *others'* doctrines in his own comparative statics terms—a feature of Ricardian monetary controversy as well as of Ricardian controversy on Say's Law and general gluts. Even though Jeremy Bentham had explicitly declared it "essential to begin by making a distinction between *immediate* causes and the more or less *remote* causes,"[124] Ricardo's criticism of Bentham's monetary theory was in strictly comparative statics terms—and in these terms Ricardo could not see how "an increase of money will call forth an addi-

---

[118] Thornton, *Paper Credit of Great Britain*, p. 152.
[119] Ibid.   [120] Ibid.; see also p. 97.
[121] Ibid., p. 250.   [122] Ibid., pp. 255–256.
[123] Ibid., p. 256.   [124] Ricardo, *Works*, III, 2–299.

tional amount of commodities,"[125] though he noted in passing that a momentary effect of this kind might be possible through wage lag and increased profitability,[126] that other "temporary" effects might occur,[127] but in general he assumed that Bentham simply "confounds the terms riches and money."[128] A similar pattern was apparent in Ricardo's polemics with Malthus and Thornton on international money movements.[129]

Perhaps the most familiar features of classical monetary theory were (1) the "quantity theory of money" and (2) the belief that money was a "veil" obscuring but not changing real variables. The real question is the substantive meanings of these two propositions, for in their pure, unqualified senses these two doctrines are incorrect individually, mutually contradictory, and inconsistent with the actual views of the classical economists.

The dominant monetary theory during the classical period was of course the quantity theory of money—but a very different theory in substance from what might be expected from the Keynesian interpretation of it. The idea that the price level usually moves in the same direction as, and at similar rates to, the quantity of money goes back much further than classical economics. The idea that the price level is *rigidly* linked to the quantity of money by a velocity of circulation which remains con-

[125] Ibid., p. 304; see also pp. 317, 325, 329, 333.
[126] Ibid., pp. 318–319.   [127] Ibid., p. 324.
[128] Ibid., p. 334.
[129] Ibid., pp. 47–127; cf. Thornton, *Paper Credit of Great Britain*, pp. 143, 151, 353; [T. R. Malthus], "Pamphlets on the Bullion Question," *Edinburgh Review*, August 1811, pp. 448–470; Ricardo, *Works*, VI, 21–42.

stant through all transitional adjustment processes cannot be found in any classical, neoclassical or modern proponent of the quantity theory of money. The changes in the velocity of circulation—short run and/or long run—were analyzed by David Hume, Adam Smith, Henry Thornton, T. R. Malthus, David Ricardo, Nassau Senior, John Stuart Mill, Alfred Marshall, Knut Wicksell, Irving Fisher, and Milton Friedman.[130] A fixed velocity of money was a straw man attacked by Keynes.[131]

The quantity theorists have postulated a relatively stable velocity over long periods of time, though with some secular trends due to evolving methods of economizing in the use of money. Short-run changes in velocity were thought of as more abrupt, and potentially catastrophic in their effects on real variables, but as predict-

[130] Hume, *Writings on Economics*, pp. 42–44; Smith, *Wealth of Nations*, pp. 306–308; Thornton, *Paper Credit of Great Britain*, pp. 233, 263, 267; [T. R. Malthus], "Tooke—on High and Low Prices," *Quarterly Review*, April 1823, p. 223; Ricardo, *Works*, III, 90; Nassau W. Senior, *Three Lectures on the Cost of Obtaining Money* (London: John Murray, 1830), pp. 57, 79, 80, and Nassau W. Senior, *Three Lectures on the Value of Money* (London: B. Fellowes, 1840), pp. 14, 16, 26; J. S. Mill, *Principles*, Toronto edn., pp. 512–514; Alfred Marshall, *Official Papers* (London: Macmillan & Co., 1926), pp. 267–268, and Alfred Marshall, *Money Credit & Commerce* (New York: Augustus M. Kelley, 1965), p. 45; Knut Wicksell, *Lectures on Political Economy* (London: Routledge & Kegan Paul, 1962), II, 59–67, 150; Irving Fisher, *The Purchasing Power of Money* (New York: Augustus M. Kelley, 1963), pp. 164, 270; Milton Friedman, *The Optimum Quantity of Money* (Chicago: Aldine Publishing Company, 1969), p. 62.

[131] John Maynard Keynes, *The General Theory of Employment, Interest and Money* (New York: Harcourt, Brace & Co., 1936), pp. 209, 289, 296.

able in theory and foreseeable in practice. Moreover, such changes did not offset changes in the quantity of money, but tended to reinforce them. A rapidly increasing quantity of money tended to reduce money holdings because of fears of its future decline in purchasing power, thereby speeding up the velocity of circulation and causing the price level to rise somewhat more rapidly than the quantity of money. Conversely, a rapidly declining quantity of money tended to produce loss of "confidence" and promoted additional precautionary money holdings, causing deflation to be accentuated.

The actual mechanisms tending to create the conditions described by the quantity theory of money were spelled out only in part during the classical period. However, there was recognition by the classical economists that the general price level rose when there were general shortages of goods at the existing prices. Similarly, there was a general price decline when more goods were supplied than demanded at existing prices. John Stuart Mill was the first major classical economist to equate an excess demand for money with an excess supply of goods, though George Poulett Scrope had done so earlier,[132] and suggestions of such a relationship are found in Robert Torrens[133] and in J. B. Say.[134] Indeed, such a relationship is implied in the many classical denials of a demand for money beyond the demand for it for transactions purposes during the current period. The *neoclassical* economists were more explicit in pointing out the inconsistency between the assertion that aggregate supply always equals

[132] See footnotes 76, 77, and 78 above.
[133] Robert Torrens, *An Essay on the Production of Wealth*, pp. 419–422.
[134] Say, *Letters to Thomas Robert Malthus*, pp. 45n–46n.

aggregate demand for goods ("Say's identity") and the quantity theory of money, which requires the possibility that aggregate supply may differ from aggregate demand, in order to change price levels.[135]

The demand for money was analyzed by the classical economists in much more detail than might be expected from individuals who sometimes wrote as if the only demand for money was a transactions demand and who strenuously denied hoarding. Here, as in other areas of monetary theory, the fullest, most incisive, and most respected[136] analysis during the classical period was that of Henry Thornton. He recognized that during "times of alarm" there is a "disposition to hoard,"[137] that a scarcity of money for some is due to larger than usual cash balances being held by others, causing "a more slow circulation" of money in general.[138] Ricardo also recognized that "alarm" could cause people to "hoard" money,[139] that money could be demanded for speculative purposes.[140] John Stuart Mill likewise said that during "a commercial crisis" the individual's demand "is specifically for money, not for commodities or capital,"[141] i.e., not simply a trans-

---

[135] Wicksell, *Lectures on Political Economy*, II, 159–160.

[136] J. S. Mill, writing more than forty years after Thornton's *Paper Credit of Great Britain*, described this work as "even now the clearest exposition" on the subject in the English language. J. S. Mill, *Principles*, Toronto edn., p. 531n. See also [T. R. Malthus], "Depreciation of Paper Money" *Edinburgh Review*, February 1811, p. 340; Sismondi, *Nouveaux Principes*, II, 83.

[137] Thornton, *Paper Credit of Great Britain*, p. 97.

[138] Ibid., p. 100.   [139] Ricardo, *Works*, III, 365.

[140] Ibid., I, 298.

[141] J. S. Mill, *Principles*, Toronto edn., p. 654.

actions demand. Robert Torrens pointed out that the usual relationship between the rate of interest did not hold at such times, that "the interest of money may rise while the profits of stock fall to nothing."[142] The demand exceeds the supply of money during a glut brought on by disproportionality, for while the increased money income of the underproducers equalled the reduced money income of the overproducers (in accordance with Say's Law), the willingness of the former to lend to the latter could be lessened: "The multiplied failures in agriculture, manufacturers, and trade, would strike a panic into the holders of floating capital, and they would refuse to grant accommodation upon securities, which in more prosperous times they would be disposed to consider unobjectionable."[143]

While McCulloch flatly denied that "gluts" were due to "a permanent deficiency of money," he nevertheless agreed that "sudden and extensive changes" in the money supply could cause "great derangement" of the economy and "may thus occasion a glut of the market, not only in the country which is the seat of the revulsion, but also in those countries whence she has been accustomed to draw any considerable portion of her supplies."[144]

The supply curve of money was conceived of quite differently by the classical economists than by modern economists. Instead of an infinitely inelastic money supply determined by monetary authorities, there was an infinitely elastic supply of gold at a national price level

[142] Torrens, *An Essay on the Production of Wealth*, p. 422.
[143] Ibid., p. 424.
[144] McCulloch, *Principles of Political Economy*, 5th edn., p. 158.

equal to that of other nations. The purchasing power of bullion was rendered equal internationally,[145] through either direct gold shipments or through paper transactions that tended to produce the same purchasing power parity. Where there was a paper currency, international price levels need not be equalized but the international purchasing power of gold still tended to be equalized— which meant that, with an inflated paper currency, the bullion price of gold would tend to exceed its value as minted money or its nominal value in paper currency.[146] Various governmental restrictions might prevent these tendencies from manifesting themselves openly, but the pressures generated would work themselves out in other ways—through the disappearance of gold coins from circulation, international smuggling, etc.

Many of the monetary controversies which raged during the classical period turned on empirical questions as to the past and present behavior of the money supply— defined variously, then as now—and as to the consequences to expect from various policies proposed. Purely theoretical controversy in the monetary field was not a feature of classical economics, though such purely theoretical discussions did occur on a considerable scale in classical value theory and in other areas. The classical economists, with their general distrust of government, tended to regard a paper currency as the road to inflation, but favored paper money in principle, if properly regu-

[145] Thornton, *Paper Credit of Great Britain*, pp. 119n, 264, 265; [Malthus], "Depreciation of Paper Money," p. 341.

[146] This is the theme of Ricardo's pamphlet *The High Price of Bullion, A Proof of the Depreciation of Bank Notes*; see Ricardo, *Works*, III, 47–127. See also J. S. Mill, *Principles*, Toronto edn., pp. 644–646.

lated, as a means of replacing gold with a far less expensive device for doing the same work.[147]

Contrary to Keynesian interpretation, the classical economists did *not* assume infinite price flexibility. No such assumption was explicit in the writings of the classical economists, and their repeated acknowledgments of important short-run changes in real variables due to monetary changes implicitly denied perfect price flexibility. As noted above, the classical economists agreed that an increased money supply could, under some short-run conditions, lower the interest rate, bring fuller utilization of capacity, and thereby increase real output. Ricardo also acknowledged that money wage rates might lag behind rising prices, causing a short-run reduction of real wage rates and a corresponding increase of the profit rate and therefore of the rate of savings and investment.[148] This was the so-called forced savings doctrine, also subscribed to by Malthus, Thornton, and Torrens,[149] among others. Correspondingly, a suddenly decreased money supply could be "disastrous" according to Ricardo,[150] and J. B. Say argued that idle money was in fact a cause of a contemporary depression.[151] Ricardo resisted the idea of downward wage rigidity which was part of

[147] Smith, *Wealth of Nations*, pp. 276, 280–281, 284; Ricardo, *Works*, IV, 43–114; ibid., VI, 69; ibid., VII, 151; ibid., VIII, 295; Torrens, *An Essay on the Production of Wealth*, pp. 320–321; J. S. Mill, *Principles*, Toronto edn., p. 642; ibid., *Collected Works*, IV, 82.

[148] Ricardo, *Works*, III, 318–319; ibid., VI, 233.

[149] [Malthus], "Depreciation of Paper Money," p. 364; Thornton, *Paper Credit of Great Britain*, p. 239; Torrens, *An Essay on the Production of Wealth*, p. 326.

[150] Ricardo, *Works*, III, 94.

[151] Say, *Letters to Thomas Robert Malthus*, pp. 45n–46n.

the Malthusian system,[152] but he cited examples of it him-self.[153] Thornton distinguished the effect of *low* prices from the effect of *falling* prices, arguing that low prices as a permanent equilibrium condition would not cause unemployment, but that a temporary fall in prices, "probably with no correspondent fall in the rate of wages," would cause unemployment and reduced national output.[154]

FISCAL POLICY

The incidence of various forms of taxation by social class and the allocational implications of these taxes were a major microeconomic concern of Ricardo and the Ricardians. Indeed, Ricardo regarded economic principles as directly useful "only" when "it directs Government to right measures in taxation."[155] This was because laissez-faire was a sufficient policy (or lack of policy) elsewhere. The unavoidable necessity of financing government activities made taxation inevitable, and raised the question of how to neutralize the effects of taxes on allocation and distribution. Adam Smith was similarly concerned with the effects of taxation, though not so preoccupied with it as the Ricardians. While the classical economists gave somewhat more attention to the microeconomic aspects of government fiscal operations than to their macroeconomic aspects, they nevertheless had important things to say on the consequences of government fiscal activities on aggregate demand, the capital stock, and employment. The dissenting economists—notably Lauderdale—had even more to say on such macroeconomic questions.

[152] Ricardo, *Works*, IX, 25.   [153] Ricardo, *Works*, VIII, 316.
[154] Thornton, *Paper Credit of Great Britain*, pp. 118–119.
[155] Ricardo, *Works*, VIII, 132–133.

The classical economists opposed deficit spending and advocated paying off the national debt, though not for any of the naïve reasons which post-Keynesian economics has concentrated on refuting. The modern doctrine that "we owe it to ourselves" was apparently current in Adam Smith's time, for *The Wealth of Nations* set out to refute the notion that revenue is merely "transferred" without the nation as a whole being "a farthing the poorer."[156] Smith argued that this was factually incorrect, since "a very considerable share in our public funds" was held by foreigners. More fundamentally, Smith and the later classical economists saw the losses from the national debt as resulting from the behavioral responses it produced in the market. Smith saw the heavier taxation made necessary by the existence of a large national debt as a serious disincentive to efficient production at home and a reason for some capital to move abroad.[157] Here Smith did not seem to consider the disincentive effects of alternative means of financing the same governmental expenditures, and in fact he apparently thought that the total expenditure would be less if the government had to go to the people for more taxes instead.

Ricardo likewise opposed deficit spending because it "tends to make us less thrifty—to blind us to our real situation."[158] "In point of economy, there is no real difference" between tax finance and bond finance, if everyone behaved with perfect rationality, despite those who "have some vague notion" that debt "would be paid by posterity."[159] He asked, "Where is the difference" if a man leaves a given fortune to his heir charged with a

[156] Smith, *Wealth of Nations*, 879.
[157] Ibid., p. 880. [158] Ricardo, *Works*, I, 247.
[159] Ibid., IV, 186–187.

given tax, or leaves a fortune free of tax, but smaller by the capitalized value of the total tax payments due.[160] Ricardo, like Smith, feared an export of capital when investors became fearful of the effects of a large national debt.[161] Like Smith he was concerned that the political advantages of deficit spending would increase the total amount spent and increase the danger of "wantonly"— both men used the same word—becoming engaged in war.[162] He added: "There cannot be a greater security for the continuance of peace than the imposing on ministers the necessity of applying to the people for taxes to support a war."[163]

The biggest challenge to classical fiscal policy came from Lord Lauderdale and was connected with his general challenge to Say's Law. Lauderdale made the argument that we owe it to ourselves,[164] that "a transfer of any given sum from the one to the other could never diminish the collective wealth of the whole,"[165] and rejected analogies between public and private debt as long as the former was an internal debt.[166] This part of his argument represented a revision of classical assumptions rather than a basic theoretical difference. The theoretical differences between Lauderdale and the classical traditions arose during their discussions of the theory of a sinking fund. The so-called sinking fund to retire the national debt, which Smith and Ricardo had denounced as

[160] Ibid., p. 187.
[161] Ibid., p. 187; ibid., I, 247–248.
[162] Ibid., IV, 186; Smith, *Wealth of Nations*, p. 878.
[163] Ricardo, *Works*, IV, 197.
[164] Lauderdale, *Three Letters*, pp. 32, 33, 34, 44, 45, 80n.
[165] Ibid., p. 33.
[166] Ibid., pp. 31, 33, 39, 77, 79, 82, 84, 85, 125, 126.

illusory,[167] and as a temptation to increased spending[168] was attacked by Lauderdale in terms of its expected effect if honestly carried out. According to the theory behind the sinking fund, a series of budgetary surpluses would be invested by the government and the interest and principal used ultimately to retire the national debt. Lauderdale argued that budgetary surpluses would in effect convert consumption expenditures into investment expenditures—"It effects the *creation* and not merely the *transfer* of capital"[169]—thereby raising the question whether there was any limit to profitable investment.

By taxing income which would otherwise have been spent (wholly or partially) on consumption, and devoting it to investment, the sinking fund scheme was one which would produce "forced accumulation, by the authority of the government,"[170] beyond the point where voluntary investment would have been forthcoming at the prevailing rate of return. The involuntary nature of this additional investment was repeatedly stressed by Lauderdale.[171] Even James Mill, in criticizing Lauderdale, acknowledged that the latter was not discussing "voluntary parsimony."[172] In the long run, of course, the same

[167] Smith, *Wealth of Nations*, p. 868; Ricardo, *Works*, I, 249; ibid., IV 194, 195.

[168] Smith, *Wealth of Nations*, pp. 868, 873; Ricardo, *Works*, IV, 193, 198.

[169] The Earl of Lauderdale, *Observations on The Review of His Inquiry into the Nature and Origin of Public Wealth, Published in the VIIIth Number of the Edinburgh Review* (Edinburgh. A. C. II. Constable & Co., 1804), pp. 75–76.

[170] Lauderdale, *Nature and Origin of Public Wealth*, p. 232.

[171] Ibid., pp. 245, 254, 267; *Three Letters*, pp. 7, 10, 68, 79, 84, 108.

[172] [James Mill], "Lord Lauderdale on Public Wealth," p. 14.

total investment (public plus private) might exist, as the private investors disinvest when the increased supply of capital forces the rate of return below their supply price. Lauderdale did not explicitly discuss this possibility, though his reference to "suddenly" changing demand patterns[173] and to the "rapidity" of forced investment, as well as his general context, suggests a short-run problem. Certainly there was no suggestion of secular stagnation in Lauderdale,[174] who accepted as indisputable that aggregate supply and aggregate demand tended to equality if left to themselves.[175]

Since Lauderdale was as convinced as Smith or Ricardo that the theory of the sinking fund would never be carried out in practice, the real thrust of his argument was directed against the classical view that there is no limit to the amount of capital. Lauderdale was the first to explore the short-run limits to sustainable investment—given declining returns to successive units of capital,[176] and, though his views were ignored or distorted by the Ricardians with their emphasis on comparative statics, the substance of his argument reappeared in its entirety in John Stuart Mill.[177]

[173] Lauderdale, *Nature and Origin of Public Wealth*, p. 245.

[174] Cf. Frank Albert Fetter, "Lauderdale's Oversaving Theory," *American Economic Review*, June 1945, p. 281.

[175] According to Lauderdale, "nothing is found more nearly commensurate than the expenditure and revenue of every society." (*Nature and Origin of Public Wealth*, p. 229.) The proposition that "the revenue and expenditure of all societies must be equivalent, if left to the natural course of things," was regarded as "so generally admitted, as to require no illustration." (*Three Letters*, p. 121.)

[176] Lauderdale, *Nature and Origin of Public Wealth*, pp. 252, 257, 263, 274.

[177] J. S. Mill, *Principles*, Toronto edn., pp. 738–739.

The contrast between the wartime prosperity in Britain during the struggle against Napoleon and the postwar depression brought on a number of reevaluations of the effect of government spending on aggregate demand. The classical doctrine that government spending was only a transfer of spending, rather than a net increment, was challenged by William Blake in 1823. He argued that sometimes liquid funds which were unavailable for private investment at the going rate of return were nevertheless available for the purchase of government bonds at the same rate of return, since the lenders "prefer the security of government to that of private borrowers,"[178] so that deficit spending represented a net increment of money demand, rather than a simple transfer. Although Blake disclaimed any attempt to show permanent growth rate increases through fiscal policy,[179] he was attacked by Ricardo, James Mill, and John Stuart Mill in essentially long-run comparative statics terms.[180] Later the younger Mill appropriated (without credit) Blake's assumption of idle capital and idle liquid hoards in the economy in his *Essays on Some Unsettled Questions in Political Economy*.[181]

SUMMARY AND CONCLUSIONS

The preoccupation of classical economics with questions of economic growth influenced their whole development

[178] William Blake, *Observations on the Effects Produced by the Expenditure of Government During the Restriction of Cash Payments* (London: John Murray, 1823), p. 62.

[179] Ibid., pp. 63, 120.

[180] Ricardo, *Works*, IV, 323–356; James Mill, *Elements of Political Economy*, p. 237 (1829 edn., p. 231); J. S. Mill, "War Expenditure," *Westminster Review*, July 1824, pp. 27–48.

[181] J. S. Mill, *Essays on Some Unsettled Questions in Political Economy*, pp. 67–72; cf. Blake, *Observations*, pp. 54, 62.

and presentation of macroeconomics. Say's Law answered those who feared that economic growth had reached, or was approaching, some ultimate limit to what the economy could profitably absorb. The central point of Say's Law was that no such limit existed, "otherwise how could it be possible that there should now be bought and sold in France five or six times as many commodities as in the miserable reign of Charles VI?"[182] The dissenters from Say's Law—Sismondi, Lauderdale, Malthus, and others— never challenged the basic proposition that markets could always be cleared or that secular growth was unlimited. They challenged another growth-related idea—that increased quantities of savings necessarily increased the growth rate. For the general glut theorists there was an equilibrium level of savings and output, beyond which declining earnings forced a retrenchment, even though at some future date, under improved technology, a larger amount of savings and/or output would be sustainable.

The role of money was also seen within a growth-related framework. A greater or smaller quantity of money made no long-run difference to the growth of real output, contrary to the mercantilists, and this was sufficient reason for the classical economists to call it a "veil" which obscures without changing reality. The continuing campaign against popular mercantilist notions led to some strong words on the neutrality of money, which were inconsistent with many classical acknowledgments of the short-run effects of money on the behavior or real variables. The possible short-run effects of fiscal policy on aggregate output were ignored or denied by shifting to a long-run perspective in which economic growth was unaffected by transfers. Short-run situations in which the

[182] Say, *A Treatise on Political Economy*, p. 137.

government's supply of investment (Lauderdale) or demand for goods (Blake) represented more than a transfer were denied by assuming that such demand could *only* be a transfer.

While the classical economists were never at their best in interpreting other viewpoints, their understanding of economic phenomena was much more sophisticated than their interpreters have allowed. Despite a penchant for dogmatic assertions, the classical economists had the saving grace of inconsistency which allowed them to recognize exceptions and modifications, and even to quietly incorporate some of the views of heretics, once orthodoxy had been vindicated.

Microeconomics

CLASSICAL allocation and distribution theory, like classical macroeconomics, reflected a preoccupation with secular growth. Despite the classical economists' many static concepts and theories, the dominating concerns to which these theories were applied were not wholly or primarily short-run problems. The *analytical* law of diminishing returns, as a static concept, was only a point of departure for discussing *historical* diminishing returns and its implications. The Ricardian scheme of functional distribution under static equilibrium was used as a basis for discussing Ricardo's real concern, the changes in distributional patterns over time[1] with economic growth and development. The short run was largely the province of dissenters during the classical period.

Classical microeconomics was as much dominated by the law of diminishing returns as classical macroeconomics was by Say's Law. Diminishing returns was not only important to the theory of rent, but was also an implicit assumption of the Malthusian population theory, and was essential in the theory of wage and profit movements over time. Classical value theory was the basic building block of the whole classical system as it was developed

[1] David Ricardo, *The Works and Correspondence of David Ricardo*, ed. Piero Sraffa (Cambridge: Cambridge University Press, 1951–55), I, 5; ibid., VIII, 278.

and presented, but the substantive theories of that system can be presented without the so-called labor theory of value. After consideration of the substance of classical microeconomics, without reference to classical value theory, it will be easier to see the reasons for the various formulations of value theory in the classical period.

DIMINISHING RETURNS

With the law of diminishing returns, as with Say's Law, modern refinements have produced an analytical principle far less ambiguous than that enunciated and disputed in the classical period. Again, as with Say's Law, this analytical clarification can be a source of historical confusion when the modern doctrine is read back into the earlier economists as the object of their discussions and debates. Classical diminishing returns meant three different things:

1. Agricultural output increased at a decreasing rate as inferior land was taken under cultivation. This was simply a tautology, since "inferior" land was inferior precisely with respect to its ability to convert inputs into output.
2. Equal successive increments of variable input added to a fixed input produced declining increments of output at a given level of technology. This approximates the modern, static, law of diminishing returns.
3. Historically, equal successive increments of labor and capital with fixed availability of arable land had produced and/or will produce declining increments of output, despite the usual technological improvements. This was the doctrine that was crucial for classical policy.

The classical economists usually did not keep their ideas on diminishing returns very distinct, but shifted from one concept to another in the middle of their analyses with relative ease and unconcern. Sometimes they treated the law of diminishing returns as referring to a declining average product,[2] sometimes to a declining marginal product,[3] sometimes to a diminishing return with given technology,[4] and sometimes to a diminished return despite technological advance.[5] Diminishing returns were thought to apply peculiarly to agriculture, while manufacturing was thought to show either constant or increasing returns. Here again there was an ambiguity: Manufacturing was sometimes said to have increasing returns to scale,[6] and sometimes to have increasing returns

[2] ". . . the whole quantity of work bestowed on land . . . extracts from the soil a gradually diminishing proportionate return." [Sir Edward West], *Essay on the Application of Capital to Land* (London: P. Underwood, 1815), p. 15; see also ibid., pp. 29, 36, 44; John Stuart Mill, *Principles of Political Economy*, Ashley edn., pp. 177, 178, 185, 427; ibid., Toronto edn., pp. 174, 175, 181, 182, 421.

[3] [West], *Essay on the Application of Capital to Land*, pp. 12, 15, 38; Ricardo, *Works*, I, 72.

[4] J. S. Mill, *Principles*, Ashley edn., p. 427; Toronto edn., p. 421.

[5] [West], *An Essay on the Application of Capital to Land*, pp. 19, 23-24; Thomas Robert Malthus, *An Inquiry into the Nature and Progress of Rent* (Baltimore: Johns Hopkins Press, 1903), pp. 36, 38; Thomas Robert Malthus, *Principles of Political Economy*, 2nd edn. (London: John Murray, 1836), pp. 195-196; Ricardo, *Works*, I, 120; John Ramsey McCulloch, *Principles of Political Economy* (Edinburgh: Adam and Charles Black, 1864), p. 414.

[6] [West], *Essay on the Application of Capital to Land*, p. 37; J. S. Mill, *Principles*, Ashley edn., p. 185; Toronto edn., p. 182.

over time.[7] However, Ricardo and McCulloch also noted that the law of diminishing returns and the determination of price by rising marginal cost may apply more generally—outside agriculture as well as within it.[8]

What was quite clear to the classical economists was the crucial importance of diminishing returns for their whole analytical system. John Stuart Mill said: "This general law of agricultural industry is the most important proposition in political economy. Were the law different, nearly all the phenomena of the production and distribution of wealth would be other than they are."[9]

Rent

Few concepts in classical economics were defined so clearly and directly as Ricardian rent: "Rent is that portion of the produce of the earth which is paid to the landlord for the use of the original and indestructible properties of the soil."[10] Yet this definition was immediately modified by Ricardo himself. Whether a payment was made to the landlord or not did not matter. With fixed leases or a tax on rent (or a society with different institutional arrangements), more or less than the rent might go to the landlord, without changing any allocational conclusions.[11] Moreover, not only the original properties of the soil but any permanent improvements yielded rent.[12] Finally, rent could apply outside agricul-

[7] J. S. Mill, loc. cit.; Malthus, *Nature and Progress of Rent*, p. 38.

[8] Ricardo, *Works*, I, 73; McCulloch, *Principles of Political Economy*, pp. 424–425.

[9] J. S. Mill, *Principles*, Ashley edn., p. 174; Toronto edn., p. 174.

[10] Ricardo, *Works*, I, 67.   [11] Ibid., p. 71.

[12] Ibid., pp. 261n–262n; see also Adam Smith, *An Inquiry into*

ture.[13] Ricardo's less often quoted definition of rent was more consistently adhered to, and was closer to the modern doctrine: ". . . rent is always the difference between the produce obtained by the employment of two equal quantities of capital and labour."[14]

It was a common expository device of the Ricardians and their popularizers to depict a successive recourse to poorer and poorer land to meet rising food needs. The poorest land cultivated at any given time would be that land whose proceeds would just cover the cost of production, including "normal profits," with nothing left over for rent. The difference between output on such no-rent land and that on superior land was rent. However, neither varying fertility nor no-rent land was necessary or sufficient for diminishing returns or rent. The assumptions of the West-Malthus-Ricardo analysis can be illustrated on a table showing output with various labor inputs on different grades of land:

	One Worker	Two Workers	Three Workers	Four Workers
Land A	10	18	24	28
Land B	9	16	21	24
Land C	8	14	18	20
Land D	7	12	15	16

Declining increments of output with increased variable inputs—reading across—were sufficient for diminishing

the *Nature and Causes of the Wealth of Nations* (New York: Modern Library, 1937), pp. 144–145.

[13] Ricardo, *Works*, I, 73; J. R. McCulloch, *Principles of Political Economy*, pp. 424–425; J. S. Mill, *Principles*, Ashley edn., pp. 476–477; Toronto edn., pp. 494–496.

[14] Ricardo, *Works*, I, 71.

returns and rent. If *all* land were *A*-quality land, both diminishing returns and rent would exist. If the price of agricultural produce were sufficient to cause two workers to be employed on land *A*, then the incremental return to the second worker—8 units—must be yielding normal earnings. Therefore the return to the first worker—10 units—must yield above normal earnings or rent. Similarly, if three are employed, the second worker's marginal product must include two units of rent and that of the first worker four units. Declining increments as poorer land was used—reading down the columns—was a prominent symptom rather than an essential feature of diminishing returns or rent. Critics who questioned whether historical land progress patterns were those of the model, or whether there really existed any no-rent land, were wide of the mark. Smith, West, Malthus, and the Ricardians all recognized that the convenience of locations affected rent,[15] and West remarked that *many* circumstances "may disturb the operation of the principle"[16] of progress to poorer soils. More importantly, recourse to poorer land merely indicated that the law of diminishing returns was *already* operating on better land.[17] If one worker is used on land *B* to produce 9 units of output, it is because the 10 units produced by the first worker on land *A* could not be duplicated by a second worker on land *A*. It "proves that additional work cannot

---

[15] Smith, *Wealth of Nations*, p. 147; [West], *Essay on the Application of Capital to Land*, pp. 13, 14; Malthus, *Nature and Progress of Rent*, pp. 21, 23; Ricardo, *Works*, I, 70; McCulloch, *Principles of Political Economy*, p. 422; J. S. Mill, *Principles*, Ashley edn., p. 433; Toronto edn., p. 428.

[16] [West], *Essay on the Application of Capital to Land*, p. 14n.

[17] Ibid., p. 14.

be bestowed with the same advantage as before on the old land."[18]

As for the no-rent land, its existence or nonexistence "is of no importance" for the principle, "for it is the same thing" if marginal increments of the variable input "yield only the return of stock with its normal profits,"[19] anything more than this being rent. In the table above, if an incremental output of 4 units per worker input yielded "ordinary profits," then four workers would be employed on land A, three workers on land B and C, and two workers on land D. Each quality of land would yield rent, equal to the difference between its yield at the no-rent *intensive* margin and the yield of its intramarginal increments of variable input. Rent would thus be 4 units on D, 6 on C, 9 on B, and 12 on A. Even if "there is never any *land* taken into cultivation" which does not yield rent, "it would be true, nevertheless, that there is always some *agricultural capital* which pays no rent,"[20] and the intramarginal returns above this measures the Ricardian rent on land.

The Ricardians clearly and consistently emphasized that rent was determined by price but was not itself a determinant of price. Price was determined by the rising cost of production at the margin. Lower cost units within the margin had no affect on price but sold for the same price as that already determined by higher cost units, thereby yielding a surplus return or rent. Ricardo was highly critical of Adam Smith, who sometimes depicted rent as price determined and sometimes as price deter-

[18] Loc. cit. [19] Ricardo, *Works*, I, 328.
[20] J. S. Mill, *Principles*, Ashley edn., p. 427; Toronto edn., p. 421.

mining.[21] However, what might appear at first as a simple case of confusion in Smith was in fact an indication of a deeper insight than the Ricardians', combined with a less rigorous use of terms.

The Ricardian model dealt with *one* agricultural commodity for simplicity. Smith's analysis took into account the *alternative* uses of the land, and treated the rent of land in one use as the necessary supply price of that same land for alternative uses.[22] In Smith's analysis, rent could even become part of the price of fish, when it was necessary to bid shore land away from its alternative uses in order to go fishing.[23] Sometimes Smith referred to the fact that rent was a "component part"[24] of price in a manner that might suggest that rent, profits, wages, etc., were independently determined and collectively determined price. Ricardo, in fact, interpreted Smith in this way.[25] However, Smith was as clear as the later classical economists that rent was in general price determined rather than price determining:

> Rent, it is to be observed, therefore, enters into the composition of the price of commodities in a different way from wages and profit. High or low wages and profit, are the causes of high or low price; high or low rent is the effect of it. It is because high or low wages and profit must be paid, in order to bring a particular commodity to market, that its price is high or low. But

[21] Smith, *Wealth of Nations*, p. 146; cf. Ricardo, *Works*, I, 67–68, 327–337.
[22] Smith, *Wealth of Nations*, pp. 150, 151, 152, 159.
[23] Ibid., p. 145.
[24] Ibid., pp. 49, 50; see also p. 248.
[25] Ricardo, *Works*, I, 329.

it is because its price is high or low; a great deal more, or very little more, or no more, than what is sufficient to pay those wages and profit, that it affords a high rent, or a low rent, or no rent at all.[26]

John Stuart Mill recognized that the economic concept of rent and the principles on which it was regulated applied outside agriculture as well as within it. Such cases "are more frequent in the transactions of industry than is commonly supposed."[27] These included patents, "superior talents for business,"[28] and in fact all economic advantages "whether natural or acquired, whether personal or the result of social arrangements,"[29] which enable one producer to make a commodity more cheaply than its cost at the price-determining margin.

Rent had important policy implications, not only to the Ricardians, but also to later and more radical groups. The historical extension of the margin of cultivation, accompanied by historically diminishing returns, implied an increasing share of rent in the national output, making landlords the passive beneficiaries of progress. The "Ricardian" rent model had its origin in the controversies over the restrictive laws which kept out foreign wheat— the so-called Corn Laws. Free importation of food and technological progress were means of reducing the need for more intensive or more extensive cultivation at higher cost, thereby reducing (or retarding the increase of) agricultural rent. Because Ricardian rent was not a factor supply price, it could be taxed or controlled without ad-

[26] Smith, *Wealth of Nations*, pp. 145–146.
[27] J. S. Mill, *Principles*, Ashley edn., p. 476; Toronto edn., p. 494.
[28] Ibid., Ashley edn., p. 477; Toronto edn., p. 495.
[29] Loc. cit.

verse effects on resource allocation and national output.[30] Ricardo and J. S. Mill recognized the great practical problems of separating pure rent from observable rental payments, which included returns on agricultural investments—investments which would not be maintained if their returns were reduced. McCulloch even doubted whether pure agricultural rent was a significant part of total agricultural rental payments, much less of the national output.[31] However, the moral indignation generated by this unearned income made it a central feature of Henry George's "single tax" (on rent) movement and of George Bernard Shaw's Fabian socialism.[32]

Profits

Diminishing returns in agriculture were central not only to the classical theory of agricultural rent but also to the classical theory of industrial profits. Here again, historical diminishing returns over time were more important than the analytical principle of diminishing returns under static conditions. Cost functions in manufacturing were considered to be different from cost functions in agriculture, not only in their shape but also in the way they shifted over time. Marginal costs in agriculture were as-

[30] Modern "rent control" laws are often based on a similar assumption, that the supply of dwelling units is relatively fixed, at least in the short run—often ignoring the auxiliary services (heat, repair, hot water, painting, etc.) which are also included in rental payments and whose supply is *not* fixed, even in the short run.

[31] McCulloch, *Principles of Political Economy*, p. 423.

[32] Henry George, *Progress and Poverty* (New York: Modern Library, n.d.), Bk. VIII, Chap. III; George Bernard Shaw, ed. *Fabian Essays in Socialism* (Garden City: Doubleday & Co., n.d.), pp. 41-42.

sumed not only to be rising, but to be rising too sharply to be offset by any expected downward shift caused by improved technology. In manufacturing, cost functions were assumed to be either constant or downward sloping, and to be shifting downward more rapidly over time as well, in response to technological and organizational improvements.[33]

While real costs of production, in terms of factor inputs, were considered to be declining over time in manufacturing, the cost of hiring the major factor of production—labor—was rising, due to the rising marginal cost of food. The net result was a secular decline in profits. A higher proportion of the total labor time of society would be required to produce the workers' own subsistence, leaving less time remaining to produce the real income of property owners—profit and rent. Since rent would claim an increasing share of output as diminishing returns forced more intensive and more extensive cultivation, the residual share of profit must fall.

In the Ricardian model, real wages remained at some culturally determined "subsistence" level, but the number of man-hours required to produce this given subsistence increased over time, due to historically diminishing returns in agriculture. Ricardo did not in fact believe that wages remained at subsistence (a stationary population wage),[34] but more "realistic" assumptions—a rising standard of living, for example—would not have changed his conclusions but only reinforced them. Ultimately the

[33] [West], *Essay on the Application of Capital to Land*, pp. 12, 37; Malthus, *Nature and Progress of Rent*, pp. 33, 38; J. S. Mill, *Principles*, Ashley edn., pp. 185–186; Toronto edn., p. 183.

[34] Ricardo, *Works*, I, 94–95.

declining rate of return on capital would reduce net investment to zero—the stationary state.[35]

If historical returns in agriculture were either constant or rising, then "the profits of stock must constantly rise in the progress of improvement."[36] This was not what was observed: "But the profits of stock are known to fall in the progress of improvement, and, therefore, neither of the first two suppositions is the fact, and labour in agriculture must, in the progress of improvement, become actually less productive."[37]

To move from the analytical principle of diminishing returns in a static model to the practical doctrine of historically diminishing returns throughout the economy in the real world would require two additional assumptions: (1) technological improvements in agriculture would not be sufficient to offset static diminishing returns, and (2) technological improvements in manufacturing would not be sufficient to offset the rising costs of labor due to diminishing returns in agriculture.

West and Ricardo both attacked Adam Smith's theory that secular declines in profit resulted from a growth of capital and the effect of competition in the factor market.[38] Smith had argued from declining profits in a particular industry, as investment in that industry increased, to declining profits in the economy as a whole as investment increased throughout the economy.[39] West and Ri-

[35] Ibid., p. 120.
[36] [West], *Essay on the Application of Capital to Land*, p. 18.
[37] Ibid., p. 24.
[38] Ibid., p. 21; Ricardo, *Works*, I, 289–290; see also J. S. Mill, *Principles*, Ashley edn., pp. 726–727; Toronto edn., pp. 734–735.
[39] Smith, *Wealth of Nations*, p. 87.

cardo pointed out that an increase of capital, output, and population would not change the *rate* of profit,[40] as distinguished from the accumulated quantity of profit. Ricardo claimed that Smith never discusses "the increasing difficulty of providing food for the additional number of labourers which the additional capital will employ."[41] Smith, however, did refer to a situation in which "the profits on stock gradually diminish" because after "the most fertile and best situated lands have been all occupied, less profit can be made by the cultivation of what is inferior both in soil and situation."[42]

Although Smith, West, and the Ricardian school (including, in this case, Karl Marx) attempted to explain a historical decline in the profit rate, there is a serious question whether there was in fact anything to explain— whether the profit rate had really declined. The interest rate had been observed to be historically declining, and the classical economists assumed some general relationship between the rate of profit and the rate of interest.[43] However, a declining risk premium as better markets developed over time may have reduced the observable gross interest rate, even though the pure interest rate and the pure rate of profit were unchanged.[44]

[40] [West], *Essay on the Application of Capital to Land*, p. 21; Ricardo, *Works*, I, 288–289.

[41] Ricardo, *Works*, I, 289.

[42] Smith, *Wealth of Nations*, pp. 92–93.

[43] Ibid., p. 339; Ricardo, *Works*, III, 25–26, 150, 374–375.

[44] [Samuel Bailey], *An Inquiry into those Principles respecting the Nature of Demand and the Necessity of Consumption Lately Advocated by Mr. Malthus* (London: R. Hunter, 1821), pp. 10–13; J. A. Schumpeter, *History of Economic Analysis* (New York: Oxford University Press, 1954), pp. 651–652.

Population

The law of diminishing returns was implicit in the Malthusian population theory, but seventeen years passed before this implication of Malthus' *Essay on Population* in 1798 was made explicit in *The Nature and Progress of Rent* in 1815. The famous arithmetic and geometric ratios (of food and population growth, respectively) are not a statement of the law of diminishing returns. They are among the great ambiguities of Malthusian thought and—since ambiguities can be difficult to refute—one of the great sources of its enduring influence. At least three different interpretations are possible for Malthus' theory of differential growth rates between food and population:

1. The theoretically possible growth rate of population is greater than the theoretically possible growth rate of food.
2. The actual growth rate of population has been (or will be) greater than the actual growth rate of food.
3. The theoretically possible growth rate of population is greater than what the actual growth rate of food has been or will be.

Once stated in this way, the first two propositions practically collapse of their own weight. Man's food consists of plants and animals, which almost all reproduce in a shorter period of time and with more numerous offspring than man. Their theoretical growth potential is of a higher geometric order than man's. If actual rather than theoretical growth rates are compared, then historically per capita food consumption has in general increased over the centuries—prior to Malthus and since Malthus—which means that food has historically been increasing faster than population.

The third proposition, though more defensible, is less meaningful by itself. Any number of earlier writers had noted man's potential for reproducing at a rate in excess of observed rates of increase in the food supply. They typically assumed that either (1) this potential would not be fully utilized, or (2) the food supply would increase faster in the future than in the past, either as a result of agricultural improvements or the additional labor inputs resulting from the population growth itself. Malthus rejected both of these assumptions. Population "invariably" increases "when there are the means of subsistence," according to Malthus.[45] Historically diminishing returns in agriculture precluded sufficient food growth to overcome population growth. (See Figure 2, below.)

In the Malthusian tableau, the "unchecked" population growth potential was greater than the population for which there was sufficient food.

Before some point in time (t_1), it was possible for population to actually grow at its potential rate, since there was sufficient food for a greater number of people than existed. Once that point was reached and the number of people equaled the number for which there was subsistence, actual increases of population (gray line) thereafter would necessarily follow the growth of the food supply. This was the empirical meaning of the Malthusian population principle, for Malthus assumed

[45] T. R. Malthus, "An Essay on the Principle of Population," 1st edn., *On Population*, ed. Gertrude Himmelfarb (New York: Random House, 1960), p. 17; see also p. 52.

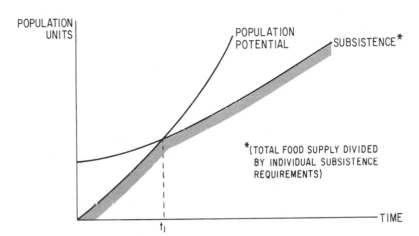

FIGURE 2

that the point t_1 had long been passed: ". . . the period when the number of men surpassed their means of subsistence has long since arrived . . . has existed ever since we have had any histories of mankind, does exist at present, and will forever continue to exist."[46] Given this clear-cut empirical proposition—that population and food grow at the *same* observable rates—it would be difficult to understand the fierce controversies which raged for decades among Malthus' contemporaries and which have been periodically revived for more than a century after his death. What was in principle an empirically resolvable question became in practice a doctrine to be salvaged by verbal shifts as the evidence piled up against it.

Two qualifications accompanied the Malthusian popu-

[46] Ibid., p. 57. This was repeated in later editions as well. See T. R. Malthus, *An Essay on the Principle of Population* (London: J. M. Dent & Sons, 1961), II, 4–5.

lation theory from the outset. Firstly, since population grew with a lag in response to favorable living conditions (food, medical care, healthy environment, etc.) and declined with a lag as such conditions deteriorated, food and population growth could be temporarily out of phase in the short run, but one could not remain above the other for any long-run period sufficient to produce a new generation whose size was adjusted to the new circumstances. There could be "oscillations"[47] around the predicted trend line, though no change in the line itself. Secondly, the unrestrained increase of population to fill out all space provided by the available subsistence was held to be a characteristic of the lower or working classes *not* shared in the higher reaches of society.[48] Although Malthus often referred to "human nature" and to "the laws of nature," his substantive analysis was in terms of differential behavior patterns in contemporary society. His openly avowed object was to vindicate such society from charges that poverty was due to institutions rather than to inherent natural causes. Malthus had little hope of solving the problem of poverty,[49] but he had hopes that his doctrine would solve the moral and political problem of assigning blame for that poverty:

> . . . it is evident that every man in the lower classes of society who became acquainted with these truths, would be disposed to bear the distresses in which he

[47] Malthus, "An Essay on the Principle of Population," *On Population*, pp. 15, 57, 162, 165n, 353, 444, 470–471.

[48] Ibid., p. 29.

[49] Ibid., p. 37; T. R. Malthus, "A Letter to Samuel Whitbread, Esq. M. P.," *An Introduction to Malthus*, ed. D. V. Glass (London: Frank Cass and Co., 1959), p. 186.

might be involved with more patience; would feel less discontent and irritation at the government and the higher classes of society, on account of his poverty. . . . The mere knowledge of these truths, even if they did not operate sufficiently to produce any marked change in the prudential habits of the poor with regard to marriage, would still have a most beneficial affect on their conduct in a political light.[50]

While the other classical economists did not share Malthus' extreme conservatism, they defended his population theory as an essential element of their system. Whatever the motivation, the defenses of the Malthusian population theory as an empirical proposition were (and are) a travesty of logic. From the fact that population is *limited* by the means of subsistence (a truism), Malthus deduced that population is *regulated* by the means of subsistence (an empirical proposition),[51] but when confronted by evidence that food was in fact growing faster than population he fell back on the potential differences, on the statement that population was somehow always "pressing" on the food supply and was "ready" to grow faster than food "whether population was *actually* increasing faster than food, or food faster than population."[52]

Sismondi, Senior, and Whately all pointed out that Malthus' use of the word "tendency" often confused an abstract potentiality with a historical trend or a statistical

[50] Malthus, "An Essay on the Principle of Population," *On Population*, pp. 591–592.

[51] Ibid., pp. 165, 337–338; Malthus, "A Summary View of the Principle of Population," *Introduction to Malthus*, p. 143.

[52] Malthus quoted in Nassau William Senior, *Two Lectures on Population* (London: Saunders and Otley, 1829), p. 61.

probability.[53] Malthus refused to be pinned down to any specific meaning. To Malthus "saying that population had a *tendency* to increase faster than the food" was not "denying that it might practically at times increase slower."[54] What he "intended to convey" was "that population was always ready, and inclined to increase faster than food, if the checks which repressed it were removed."[55] But he brushed aside Sismondi's objection that he was comparing an abstract potentiality of *A* with concrete data on *B*.

In his *Principles of Political Economy* (1820), Malthus agreed that higher incomes among workers might lead to either of "two very different results"—increase of population or "improvements in the modes of subsistence"[56]—that is subsistence might grow faster than the population or at the same rate as population. Such statements continued to coexist with other statements about "the tendency in population fully to keep pace with the means of subsistence,"[57] and statements that "the average rate of the *actual* increase of population" must be one "obeying the same laws as the increase of food"[58]—without which he had no empirical proposition at all.

[53] J.C.L. Simonde de Sismondi, *Nouveaux Principes d'économie politique*, 3rd edn., (Geneva-Paris: Edition Jeheber, 1953), II, 182; Richard Whately, *Introductory Lectures on Political Economy*, 2nd edn., (London: B. Fellows, 1832), pp. 248–250; Senior, *Two Lectures on Population*, pp. 36, 56, 58, 77.

[54] Malthus quoted in Senior, *Two Lectures on Population*, p. 60.

[55] Ibid., p. 61.

[56] Malthus, *Principles of Political Economy*, 2nd edn., p. 226.

[57] Malthus, "An Essay on the Principle of Population," *On Population*, p. 454.

[58] Malthus, "A Summary View of the Principle of Population," *An Introduction to Malthus*, p. 143.

By the time that John Stuart Mill's *Principles* was published in 1848, a substantial body of data and of blatantly obvious observations made it clear that subsistence had been increasing faster than the population for some time. This caused some economists to reject or abandon the Malthusian theory. But the support of Mill's great treatise revived it and gave it a new lease on life, despite Mill's own damaging admission:

> Subsistence and employment in England have never increased more rapidly than in the last 40 years, but every census since 1821 showed a smaller proportional increase of population than that of the period preceding; and the produce of French agriculture and industry is increasing in a progressive ratio, while the population exhibits in every quinquennial census, a smaller proportion of births to the population.[59]

This did not prevent Mill from supporting the Malthusian population theory both as a theory of potential growth rates—the "power of increase" and the "capacity of multiplication" of population being used by Mill[60]— and as a theory of actual behavior in which "improvements in the condition of the labouring classes" give only "a temporary means" of prosperity, "speedily filled up by an increase of their numbers."[61] The objections of critics to shifting Malthusian concepts which evaded empirical confrontation were brushed aside by Mill as corrections of "mere language" which did not change the real problem, that population pressed "too" closely

[59] J. S. Mill, *Principles*, Ashley edn., p. 161; Toronto edn., p. 159.
[60] Ibid., Ashley edn., p. 157; Toronto edn., pp. 154, 155.
[61] Ibid., Ashley edn., p. 161; Toronto edn., p. 159.

on the means of subsistence, bearing "too" great a ratio to capital,[62] that there was not "enough" improvement in living standards.[63]

Malthus' ultimate triumph was in *identifying* poverty with "over"-population, so that to deny the latter was considered synonymous with denying the former, and continues to be, in the eyes of many. He set a pattern by relying heavily on extrapolations and truisms that serve as impregnable refuges during critical attacks and as bases for empirical sorties at other times. Malthus' heavy emphasis on empiricism in all areas of economics did not imply a systematic *testing* of empirically verifiable hypotheses by facts. He regarded his population theory as "incontrovertible,"[64] so that history would "elucidate the manner"[65] of its operation, rather than reveal *whether* it was empirically correct. The massive empirical material added to the second edition of the *Essay on Population* was intended to be used to "examine the effects of one great cause"[66]—the population principle—rather than to test that principle itself. No matter what the population might be, it was consistent with his principle: "The natural tendency to increase is everywhere so great that it will generally be easy to account for the height at which the population is found in any country."[67]

Modern apologists for Malthus have argued that technological progress in the West has "postponed" the Malthusian result, while exploding population growth in

---

[62] Ibid., Ashley edn., p. 359; Toronto edn., pp. 353–354.
[63] J. S. Mill, *Collected Works*, IV, 449.
[64] Malthus, "An Essay on the Principle of Population," *On Population*, p. 17.
[65] Ibid., pp. 16, 163.　　　　[66] Ibid., p. 151.
[67] Ibid., p. 212.

the poorer or "underdeveloped" countries vindicates his prediction. But if population growth is regulated by the food supply or by the potential cost of production in agriculture, then it is precisely the West which should have the more rapidly increasing population. In Figure 2, the food supply curve should be rising more rapidly over time, with population correspondingly higher. Moreover, it is even questionable whether "over"-population in any meaningful sense is associated with national poverty, given that there are affluent nations, poor nations, and medium-income nations which have heavy population density, medium population density, and thin population density. It is of course true that any nation will have higher per capita income with fewer people, assuming (implicitly) that its output does not decline in proportion. But this is a statement about the rules of arithmetic rather than about any empirical reality.

Laws of Production and Distribution

John Stuart Mill attempted to show how laws of production, such as the law of diminishing returns, were "strongly distinguished" from laws of income distribution. The laws of production "partake of the character of physical truths," according to Mill. "There is nothing optional or arbitrary in them."[68] They are determined "by the constitution of external things," and by "the inherent properties" of human beings. By contrast, the distribution of output "is a matter of human institution solely."[69] Once things have been produced, "mankind, individually or

[68] J. S. Mill, *Principles*, Ashley edn., p. 199; Toronto edn., p. 199.
[69] Ibid., Ashley edn., p. 200; Toronto edn., p. 199.

collectively, can do with them what they like"[70]—placing them "at the disposal of whomsoever they please, and on whatever terms."[71] It is all a matter of "the laws and customs of society," "the feelings and opinions" of its ruling elements, and is "very different in different ages and countries" and can vary still further "if mankind so chooses."[72]

Taken very literally, Mill's words might suggest that production is a matter of economics while distribution is a matter of social philosophy. Obviously production and distribution cannot be so completely independent of each other when the manner in which a given period's output is distributed affects the use of inputs—and therefore output—in subsequent periods. Mill was well aware of this:

> We have here to consider, not the causes, but the consequences, of the rules according to which wealth may be distributed. Those, at least, are as little arbitrary, and have as much the character of physical laws, as the laws of production. Human beings can control their own acts, but not the consequences of their acts to themselves or to others. Society can subject the distribution of wealth to whatever rules it thinks best: but what practical results will flow from the operation of those rules, must be discovered, like any other physical or mental truths, by observation and reasoning.[73]

The original distinction between laws of production and laws of distribution thus collapses. In the same sense

[70] Loc. cit.
[71] Ibid., Ashley edn., p. 200; Toronto edn., pp. 199–200.
[72] Ibid., Ashley edn., p. 200; Toronto edn., p. 200.
[73] Ibid., Ashley edn., pp. 200–201; Toronto edn., p. 200.

in which society may distribute as it pleases and take the consequences, it may also produce as it pleases and take the consequences. In substance, Mill does not postulate any greater freedom in one area than in the other.

The law of diminishing returns was not only the great classical law of production, it was also the great underlying principle of functional distribution as well. Its most obvious role was in the theory of rent, but together with the theory of an infinitely elastic long-run supply of labor it also determined wages, and therefore profits as a residual. Labor supply was infinitely elastic with respect to real income, but diminishing returns made the cost of given wage goods rise over time, so that the supply curve of labor was rising with respect to the labor cost of wage goods. Rising wage and rent shares over time meant a declining profit share—and together with the rising accumulation of capital, this meant a declining profit rate.

VALUE

Although value theory may be in some sense basic or logically prior to other aspects of microeconomics, classical value theory is more readily understood after some acquaintance with the substance and purpose of classical economics in general.

For example, the classical economists ignored a substantial body of earlier and contemporary economic literature which stressed the role of utility and demand in value theory, and gave almost exclusive emphasis to cost of production or labor. This is understandable, *given* the classical assumption of statically constant cost functions in manufacturing, so that no changes in demand could change value. $P_1 = AC$, regardless of demand (D_1, D_2, D_3):

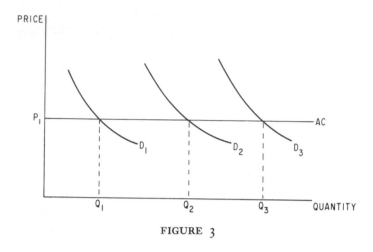

FIGURE 3

The demand for (the utility of) the product might be insufficient to cover its cost of production, in which case this particular product would not be produced in the long run. Such unproduced products were outside the purview of classical economics. Smith *defined* effective demand to mean only that quantity demanded (Q_1, Q_2, Q_3) at a price sufficient to at least cover production costs.[74] Utility and demand were therefore necessary, but not sufficient, to determine value. The actual level of value was determined by "the" cost of production. Only in cases where a monopolist maximized price, selling only one unit, would the utility determine the price. Utility in this context did not mean marginal utility but the highest average utility—the utility of having the commodity at all. And in this sense utility was "only the limit of value,"[75] not a determinant of value.

[74] Smith, *Wealth of Nations*, p. 56.
[75] J. S. Mill, *Collected Works*, IV, 400; J. S. Mill, *Principles*, Ashley edn., p. 449; Toronto edn., p. 468.

98

Measures of Value

Classical value theory dealt not only with narrow questions of price determination in particular markets but also with such broader questions as the functional distribution of income over time, the measurement of aggregate output, and changing relative prices between agricultural and manufactured goods over time. In short, classical "value" concepts ranged beyond problems of individual product price determination to problems of *measuring* or valuing output for various purposes. One such purpose was that of providing an index of welfare. Unlike the mercantilists, who measured the prosperity of a nation by its accumulated stock of gold, Adam Smith measured national prosperity by its annual flow of per capita income[76]—to be maximized by efficient production at home and free trade abroad. As a welfare index, output was to be measured by how much labor it could command: "What every thing is really worth to the man who has acquired it, and who wants to dispose of it or exchange it for something else, is the toil and trouble which it can save to himself, and which it can impose on other people."[77]

At a given time, under given technology, an index of the amount of "other men's labour" is the same as an index of "the produce of other men's labour,"[78] and from this Smith drifted into using the terms synonymously over time and without regard to changing technology. However, more fundamentally, Smith saw the utility of goods to be indicated by the disutility of labor to which their consumers will submit to obtain them:

[76] Smith, *Wealth of Nations*, p. lvii.
[77] Ibid., p. 30.   [78] Ibid., p. 31.

Equal quantities of labour, at all times and places, may be said to be of equal value to the labourer. In his ordinary state of health, strength and spirits; in the ordinary degree of his skill and dexterity, he must always lay down the same portion of his ease, his liberty and his happiness. The price which he pays must always be the same, whatever may be the quantity of goods which he receives in return for it. Of these, indeed, it may sometimes purchase a greater and sometimes a smaller quantity; but it is their value which varies, not that of the labour which purchases them. At all times and places that is dear which is difficult to come at, or which it costs much labour to acquire and that cheap which is to be had easily, or with very little labour. Labour alone, therefore, never varying in its own value, is alone the ultimate and real standard by which the value of all commodities can at all times and places be estimated and compared. It is their real price; money is their nominal price only.[79]

This defines a *measure* of value, but it is not a *theory* of value. No substantive proposition in *The Wealth of Nations* would be different if Smith had chosen a different index of welfare. Indeed, Smith chose a different measure of value in a "popular sense" on the same page and alternated between the two usages throughout the book. His "real" sometimes meant the quantity of labor command represented and sometimes the volume of physical output.[80]

Similarly, Ricardo's quest for an "invariable measure of value" was a search for a product whose cost structure

[79] Ibid., p. 33.
[80] Ibid., pp. 30, 33, 78, 159, 247, 248.

was such that changes in *other* products' costs of production over time could be directly determined by observing how they exchanged with the invariable standard,[81] much as the length or weight of an object could be directly measured by a ruler or a scale, without reference to the whole range of other objects having length and weight. Such a measure of value would show, for example, that agricultural goods were rising in value (cost) over time, while manufactured goods were falling. As John Stuart Mill observed, "Under the name of a measure of value," some economists had developed what "would be more properly termed a measure of cost of production."[82] For the Ricardians this was true. More generally, it was a measure of whatever was considered important in a policy area.

For example, Malthus' measure of value was a measure of "labour command"[83]—in keeping with his emphasis on macroeconomic unemployment problems. For Malthus, "the power of commanding a given quantity of labour of a given character, together with the will to advance it, represents a given demand."[84] When the output of a given period failed to command enough labor to reproduce the same output in subsequent periods, aggregate demand was said to be deficient. Goods are overproduced when "they are selling at a price which will not repur-

[81] See Ricardo, *Works*, I, 14, 17–18, 29, 43–44; [Samuel Bailey], *A Critical Dissertation on the Nature, Measure and Causes of Value* (London: R. Hunter, 1826), pp. 9, 121–122.

[82] J. S. Mill, *Principles*, Ashley edn., p. 566; Toronto edn., pp. 578–579.

[83] Malthus, *Principles of Political Economy*, p. 82; see also Thomas Robert Malthus, *Definitions in Political Economy* (London: John Murray, 1827), p. 210n.

[84] Malthus, *Definitions in Political Economy*, p. 52.

chase the quantity of labour employed in producing them."[85]

One of the great problems in understanding Marxian value is that it is entirely a *measure* of value rather than a *theory* of value. Marx had what he himself called a "definition of value,"[86] a "concept of value,"[87] and value "as defined."[88] He was flabbergasted at critics' "nonsense" about "proving" his concept,[89] and found it sufficient for his purposes that the allocation and distribution of labor time was a vital phenomenon in the economy.[90]

Malthus, Ricardo, and Mill all recognized that any specific, empirical measure of value was arbitrary,[91] and ultimately had to be justified by its usefulness rather than its logic alone. This was implicit also in Marx's justifications—not proofs—of his value concept. This did not

[85] Malthus, *Definitions in Political Economy*, p. 52.

[86] Karl Marx and Frederick Engels, *Selected Correspondence* (New York: International Publishers, 1942), p. 232.

[87] Ibid., p. 246.

[88] Karl Marx, *Capital* (Chicago: Charles H. Kerr & Co., 1906), I, 45.

[89] "The nonsense about the necessity of proving the concept of value arises from complete ignorance both of the subject dealt with and of the method of science." Marx and Engels, *Selected Correspondence*, p. 246.

[90] "Every child knows that a country which ceased to work, I will not say for a year, but for a few weeks, would die. Every child knows too that the mass of products corresponding to the different needs require different and quantitatively determined masses of the total labour of society. That this necessity of distributing social labour in definite proportions cannot be done away with . . . is self-evident." Loc. cit.

[91] T. R. Malthus, *The Measure of Value* (New York: Kelley & Millman, 1957), p. 16; Malthus, *Principles of Political Economy*, pp. 94–95; Ricardo, *Works*, I, 43–44; J. S. Mill, *Principles*, Ashley edn., p. 566; Toronto edn., p. 579.

prevent lengthy controversies between Ricardo and Malthus as to the best measure of value, for their general systems were oriented toward different questions—Ricardo tracing the changing functional distribution of income over time and its implications (the stationary state, for example), and Malthus concerning himself with the short-run behavior of aggregate output and employment.

The classical economists admitted that there was no perfect empirical embodiment of the concept of an invariable measure of value. Samuel Bailey went beyond this to assert that it was *conceptually* as well as empirically impossible to have such a thing. Bailey's *Critical Dissertation on the Nature, Measures, and Causes of Value* (1826) insisted repeatedly that the nature of value was wholly relative, so that it was "contradictory" to speak of "an invariable standard of value amidst universal fluctuation,"[92] for no goods could even conceivably remain constant in value as all other goods varied. He recognized that what the Ricardians were seeking, under the label of a "measure" of value was in fact "to determine in which commodity any changes of value have originated."[93] This was not, for him, a measure of value in any sense analogous to measuring weight. The third part of Bailey's title—the *causes* of value—dealt with the theory of value, which he was the first to clearly separate from the other two features of classical value with which it was usually confused.

Theory of Value

However much the classical economists differed among themselves as to the best measure of value, they were sub-

[92] [Bailey], *A Critical Dissertation on the Nature, Measures, and Causes of Value*, p. 55.
[93] Ibid., p. 127n.

stantially united on the theory of value. The cost of production determined the value of those goods with which classical economics was preoccupied—competitively sold commodities produced at constant cost. Commodities produced at increasing cost sold at their marginal cost.[94] Commodities sold in noncompetitive markets and commodities in fixed supply sold at prices determined by supply and demand.[95] Samuel Bailey pointed out that all apparent differences among his contemporaries on this point were merely differences in the use of words.[96] John Stuart Mill also stated this to be the substantive theory of *all* economists—"from Ricardo down"[97]—on the subject.

Supply and demand was, in one sense, a general mechanism through which any particular determinant of value operated. It was consistent with utility, cost of production, and other theories of price determination. "You say supply and demand regulates value," Ricardo wrote to Malthus. "This, I think, is saying nothing,"[98] since it is equally compatible with one theory or another. In another sense, however, price determination by supply and

[94] [Bailey], *A Critical Dissertation on the Nature, Measures, and Causes of Value*, pp. 185ff; [Samuel Bailey], *Observations on Certain Verbal Disputes in Political Economy* (London: R. Hunter, 1821), pp. 8off; Ricardo, *Works*, I, 74, J. S. Mill, *Principles*, Ashley edn., p. 471; Toronto edn., p. 490.

[95] Malthus, *Principles of Political Economy*, 2nd edn., p. 70; Ricardo, *Works*, I, 384; J. S. Mill, *Principles*, Ashley edn., p. 449; Toronto edn., p. 469.

[96] [Bailey], *A Critical Dissertation on the Nature, Measures, and Causes of Value*, p. 199; [Bailey], *Observations on Certain Verbal Disputes in Political Economy*, p. 82.

[97] J. S. Mill, *Collected Works*, IV, 398.

[98] Ricardo, *Works*, VIII, 279.

demand meant that there was no other specific principle at work—the competitive market was not operating as required by general theory—and prices were whatever the market happened to make them. In this sense, J. S. Mill could say that supply and demand determined prices "in cases where cost of production is inoperative,"[99] depicting supply-and-demand and cost-of-production as mutually exclusive and jointly exhaustive,[100] even though elsewhere he depicted supply and demand as an all-encompassing phenomenon through which all particular determinants of value produced their concrete results: "nothing else has any influence whatever, except in as far as it may be calculated to effect either the demand or the supply."[101]

In short, Ricardian economics regarded supply and demand as a causally neutral mechanism—like neutral money—through which *other* variables determined value. Supply and demand independently determine the value only where the other determinants (cost of production, utility) were rendered ineffective by noncompetitive market structures or fixed supply.

The terms "supply" and "demand," as used by Ricardo and John Stuart Mill referred exclusively to *quantities* supplied and demanded.[102] As Ricardo wrote to Malthus:

[99] "Wherever cost of production does *not* regulate the price there demand and supply *do* regulate it." J. S. Mill, *Collected Works*, IV, 400.

[100] Ibid., p. 33.

[101] J. S. Mill, *Collected Works*, IV, 33; see also ibid., V, 635.

[102] Ricardo, *Works*, I, 382; VI, 129; J. S. Mill, *Principles*, Ashley edn., pp. 446, 447, 449; Toronto edn., pp. 466, 467, 469; John Stuart Mill, "Notes on N. W. Senior's *Political Economy*," *Economica*, August 1945, pp. 134, 145.

I sometimes suspect that we do not attach the same meaning to the word demand. If corn rises in price, you perhaps attribute it to a greater demand,—I should call it a greater competition. The demand cannot I think be said to increase if the quantity consumed be diminished, altho much more money may be required to purchase the smaller than the larger quantity. If it were to be asked what the demand was for port wine in England in the years 1813 and 1814, and it were to be answered that in the first year she had imported 5000 pipes and in the next 4500 should we not all agree that the demand was greater in 1813, yet it might be true that double the quantity of money was paid for the 4500 pipes.[103]

While Ricardo would say that demand had declined from 1813 to 1814, Malthus would say—with modern economics (Figure 4)—that demand had increased. Defi-

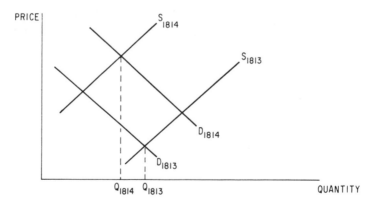

FIGURE 4

[103] Ricardo, *Works*, VI, 129.

nitions, as such, are neither "right" nor "wrong," but conflicting definitions made it difficult for these contemporaries to understand each other, or for classical statements about demand to be understood by later interpreters steeped in a different concept. Malthus, by contrast, presented the earliest *schedule* concept of supply and demand. He distinguished the "extent" (quantity) of the demand from the "intensity" of demand (height of the demand curve): ". . . it is not in the sense of mere extent of consumption that demand raises prices, because it is almost always when prices are the lowest, that the extent of demand and consumption is the greatest."[104] The "intensity" of demand was defined as "the sacrifice which the demanders are able and willing to make in order to satisfy their wants. It is this species of demand alone which, compared with the supply, determines prices and values."[105] The meaning of an increased demand in these terms was clear:

Now this willingness, on the part of some of the demanders, to make a greater sacrifice than before, in order to satisfy their wants, is what I have called a greater intensity of demand. As no increase of price can possibly take place, unless the commodity be of such a nature as to excite in a certain number of purchasers this species of demand, and as this species of demand must always be implied whenever we speak of demand and supply as determining prices.[106]

Samuel Bailey phrased Malthus' theory even more directly in modern terms: "A disposition to give more for

[104] Malthus, *Principles of Political Economy*, 2nd edn., p. 68.
[105] Malthus, *Definitions in Political Economy*, p. 245.
[106] Malthus, *Principles of Political Economy*, 2nd edn., pp. 65n–66n.

the quantity actually taken, or to buy more at the same rate"[107]—a shift outward of the demand schedule. Supply was similarly regarded by Malthus in schedule terms, as the "conditions of the supply,"[108] meaning the cost of production.[109] Malthus saw the traditional classical cost-of-production theory of value as only a special case of supply and demand theory, the more general theory being applicable to both short-run ("market") and long-run ("natural") prices, and to monopolized as well as competitively produced commodities.[110]

As in other areas of economics, advances in value theory which burst through the confines of the Ricardian system were opposed and obliterated by the appearance of Mill's *Principles* in 1848 and its dominance for the next several decades. The pattern was the familiar one of interpreting others' ideas in Ricardian senses—supply and demand being *quantities* supplied and demanded—and showing their inconsistencies in such terms.[111] What Jevons called "the noxious influence of authority" was sufficient to bury ideas not understood by the Ricardian school.[112] Mill's closed mind on the subject of value was

[107] [Bailey], *Observations on Certain Verbal Disputes in Political Economy*, p. 65.

[108] Malthus, *Principles of Political Economy*, 2nd edn., pp. 71, 73, 74; T. R. Malthus, *The Measure of Value* (London: John Murray, 1823), pp. 17, 19.

[109] Malthus, *Definitions in Political Economy*, p. 242.

[110] Malthus, *Principles of Political Economy*, 2nd edn., pp. 65n–66n, 72; Malthus, *Definitions in Political Economy*, p. 221; Malthus, *Measure of Value*, p. 44.

[111] J. S. Mill, *Principles*, Ashley edn., pp. 445, 446, 448; Toronto edn., pp. 465, 466, 467.

[112] W. Stanley Jevons, *The Theory of Political Economy* (New York: Kelley & Millman, 1957), p. 275.

evident from his youthful disparagement of "Malthus' insignificant disputes about 'value' "[113] to his more celebrated statement of his later years: "Happily, there is nothing in the laws of Value which remains for the present or any future writer to clear up; the theory of the subject is complete."[114]

SUMMARY AND CONCLUSIONS

The major substantive features of classical microeconomics revolved around the law of diminishing returns. Ricardian rent theory was obviously dependent upon it, for diminishing returns produced rent even without recourse to inferior land, and such recourse was itself evidence of already diminished returns on the superior land. Malthusian population growth presented a problem of maintaining living standards only if the additional labor input represented by the additional population did not lead to correspondingly increased increments of output. The general profit rate was likewise determined by rising marginal costs in agriculture, which raised the principal cost (food) of the principal input (labor) in manufacturing. The static law of diminishing returns was the foundation of a whole system of analysis that depended upon *historically* diminishing returns, driving up the cost of labor, increasing the landlord's rent, driving down the rate of profit, and moving the economy toward the "stationary state." In this sense, the law of diminishing returns was part of the general classical preoccupation with the problem of long-run growth.

Classical value theory was, in itself, a straightforward cost-of-production theory. The value of competitively

[113] J. S. Mill, *Collected Works*, IV, 30.
[114] J. S. Mill, *Principles*, Ashley edn., p. 436; Toronto edn., p. 456.

produced commodities equaled "the" (fixed) cost of production in manufacturing and a rising cost of production in agriculture. Since rent was not part of the cost of production, the latter reduced to the cost of capital and labor. Capital was considered to come "originally" in some historical sense or "ultimately" in some analytical sense from labor, so that cost and value would essentially be reducible to labor. For all the controversy generated by the "labor theory of value" it was tangential to classical value theory, and seldom was it even alleged that any substantive conclusion would be different without it. Ricardo's elaborate catalog of modifications of the labor theory make it quite clear that he understood the role of capital, of time, etc., in the price-determination process.[115] Such disciples as McCulloch and James Mill might, in the heat of polemics, become more Ricardian than Ricardo in insisting on the ultimate role of labor, but Ricardo himself chided them for going as far as they sometimes did.[116] Marx devoted a whole volume (Vol. II) of *Capital* to the extensive modifications of the labor theory of value necessitated by varying capital turnover, before finally going full circle to the classical cost of production theory of price determination (Vol. III).

In addition to a substantive *theory* of value, classical economics spawned a number of "measures" of value, adapted to divergent purposes, from dealing with changing costs over time (Ricardo) to analyzing cyclical unemployment (Malthus). While the validity of the whole concept of a "measure" of value, and particularly an invariable measure of value, could be challenged—as it was by Samuel Bailey—once a concept was accepted, the

[115] Ricardo, *Works*, I, Chap. I.
[116] Ibid., IX, 127, 178.

particular measure chosen could not be challenged on the grounds of validity but only on grounds of convenience.

Supply and demand were conceived of in quantity rather than schedule terms, and "utility" meant average rather than marginal utility, so the potentialities of these concepts were lost on the central classical tradition. They had later to be rediscovered and developed as if their early exponents had never existed.

CHAPTER IV

Methodology

CLASSICAL ECONOMICS in itself contained relatively little in the way of separate, explicit, methodological discussion, and most of that appeared late, in the writings of John Stuart Mill. However, methodological pronouncements were scattered through earlier classical writings, especially Ricardo's controversies with Malthus and his *Reply to Bosanquet* on monetary policy. Moreover, the implicit methodology of classical economics—and especially of the Ricardian school—gave rise to a voluminous critical literature. Even Adam Smith, whose *Wealth of Nations* said nothing about methodology, became in retrospect an important methodological figure repeatedly invoked by later critics of the Ricardians.

The methodological questions at issue during the classical period were very similar to those that were later to agitate neoclassical and modern economists. The controversies in classical methodology included (1) abstractions versus "reality," (2) varying concepts of causation, (3) the role of mathematics, (4) the "scientific" claims of economics, and (5) the practical relevance of classical economics. But before proceeding to analyze these topics, it may be worthwhile to briefly consider the historical development of classical methodology.

Adam Smith's methodology was eclectic. The empirical, the theoretical, the institutional, the philosophical, the static, and the dynamic were all intermingled. His definitions shifted, sometimes on the same page,[1] and, in the course of developing his classic work, he drifted back and forth between different conceptions of "value,"[2] "rent,"[3] and "real."[4] But, despite the numerous ambiguities in *The Wealth of Nations* commented on by Smith's classical successors,[5] as well as by the later scholars,[6] he moved easily around the pitfalls without disaster, being sufficiently consistent during any given chain of reasoning to avoid errors in logic.

With Ricardo economics took a major step toward abstract models, rigid and artificial definitions, syllogistic reasoning—and the direct application of the results to policy. The historical, the institutional, and the empirical faded into the background, and explicit social philosophy shrank to a few passing remarks. Comparative statics became the dominant—though usually implicit—approach. Ricardo declared: "I put these immediate and temporary effects quite aside, and fixed my whole attention on the

---

[1] Adam Smith, *An Inquiry into the Nature and Causes of the Wealth of Nations* (New York: Modern Library, 1937), pp. 30, 33.

[2] Ibid.

[3] Ibid. Rent was sometimes price determined (p. 56) and sometimes price determining (p. 146).

[4] Ibid. Real meant goods and services on p. 78 but labor command on pages 30, 33, 159, 247, 248.

[5] David Ricardo, *The Works and Correspondence of David Ricardo*, ed. Piero Sraffa (Cambridge: Cambridge University Press, 1951-55), I, 16-17, 19-20, 67-68; John Stuart Mill, *Principles of Political Economy*, Ashley edn., pp. 436-437, 567, 726-727. Ibid., Toronto edn., pp. 456, 580, 734-735.

[6] J. A. Schumpeter, *History of Economic Analysis* (New York: Oxford University Press, 1951), pp. 189-191 passim.

113

permanent state of things which will result from them."[7] Not only Ricardo, but his disciples and popularizers reasoned in comparative static terms, and they automatically interpreted the theories of others in comparative static terms as well.

The Ricardian approach did not remain unchallenged. A host of critics attacked from many directions, raising in the process fundamental and enduring questions of economic methodology.

SCIENCE

The attempt of the Ricardians to make economics more "scientific" met with both opposition and derision. Richard Jones objected that economics was a field in which "premeditated experiments" could seldom be made,[8] and denounced "the too hasty creation of whole systems" based on "a frail thirst for a premature exposition of commanding generalities."[9] Those who "snatched at general principles" ended up with principles which "will often be found to have no generality"[10] in the sense of having no historical setting in which they are literally true. Jones was concerned with "things as they exist in the world,"[11] with "institutions,"[12] with "history and statistics,"[13] and had no use for "closet philosophers"[14] or their "puerile effort to make reasoning supply

[7] Ricardo, *Works*, VII, 120.
[8] Richard Jones, *An Essay on the Distribution of Wealth* (London: John Murray, 1831), p. xx.
[9] Ibid., p. xxxix.
[10] Richard Jones, *Literary Remains*, ed. William Whewell (London: John Murray, 1859), p. 569.
[11] Ibid., p. 600.   [12] Ibid., p. 576.
[13] Ibid., p. 570.   [14] Ibid., p. 570.

the place of knowledge."[15] Jones was seconded by his literary executor, William Whewell, who contrasted Jones's historical and institutional analysis of rent with that of Ricardo:

But yet, as opinions are brought out most distinctly by their opposition, I may notice some of the remarks made at the time, by Mr. Ricardo's admirers, upon Mr. Jones's conclusions, and upon his reasonings. "Mr. Ricardo (they replied) does not pretend to give an exposition of the laws by which the rise and progress of rent, *in the ordinary and vulgar sense of the word*, is regulated. He was as well aware as Mr. Jones, or any one else that the rent, the origin and progress of which he had undertaken to investigate, was not that which is commonly called *rent*. He did not profess to examine the circumstances which practically determined the actual amount of rent in any country."

To this it was a sufficient reply to say, that the object of Mr. Jones *was* to give an account of the laws by which rent, "in the ordinary and vulgar sense of the word," is regulated. He tried to ascertain the progress and consequences of "what is commonly called rent." And the reader might be left to decide for himself which subject of inquiry may be the better worth his notice,—the rents that are actually paid in *every* country, or the Ricardian rents, which are *not* those actually paid in *any* country.

. . . Were not these *landholders* intended by Mr. Ricardo, and understood by all his readers, to be identified with the receivers of actual rent? or were they different from landholders "in the ordinary and

[15] Jones, *Distribution of Wealth*, p. 325.

vulgar sense of the word?" And when these disciples of his took credit to themselves, as they did, for avoiding his errors, and enforcing the identity of interest of the landlord with that of the public, who were *their* landlord, and what his interest? Was he the receiver of "what is commonly called rent," or was he an imaginary personage whose interest depends on the increase of rents "which are not paid in any country?" Was he, in short, the squire of the parish, or the creature of a definition?[16]

While most critics did not go as far as Jones and Whewell, many took similar positions on particular points. Malthus attacked the "tendency to premature generalization,"[17] and declared that before "the shrine of truth, as discovered by facts and experience, the fairest theories and the most beautiful classifications must fall."[18] Sismondi accused Ricardo of inhabiting "a hypothetical world altogether different from the real world,"[19] assuming that "a perfect equilibrium is always maintained,"[20] and "making abstraction of time and space like the German metaphysicians."[21] J. B. Say ultimately turned against the Ricardians' "method of investigation,"

[16] William Whewell, "Prefatory Notice," Richard Jones, *Literary Remains*, pp. xii–xiii.
[17] Thomas Robert Malthus, *Principles of Political Economy* (New York: Augustus M. Kelley, 1951), 2nd edn., p. 8.
[18] Ibid., p. 6.
[19] J.C.L. Simonde de Sismondi, *Nouveaux Principes d'économie politique*, 2nd edn. (Geneva-Paris: Edition Jeheber, 1951), II, 256.
[20] Ibid., I, 234.
[21] Ibid., II, 283; J.C.L. Simonde de Sismondi, *Etudes sur l'économie politique* (Paris: Treutgel et Wurtz, 1837–38), I, 85n–86n.

their "vain subtleties,"[22] and "abstract principles,"[23] saying, "It is better to stick to facts and their consequences than to syllogisms."[24]

The validity of the claim of economics to be a science depended upon what was conceived to be the distinguishing feature of a science. To some a science was characterized by the precision and rigor of its *methods of analysis*; to others a science was distinguished by the *certainty of its results*. Even when critics were prepared to use the word "science" in a loose sense to describe economics, they emphasized that "the science of political economy bears a nearer resemblance to the science of morals and politics than to that of mathematics."[25] Mathematics and the natural sciences were repeatedly contrasted with economics.[26] The widespread aversion to the use of mathematics in economics during the classical period was based on a belief that "arithmetical computations" could not be made with any certainty.[27] There was no

[22] Jean-Baptiste Say, *Œuvres diverses de J.-B. Say* (Paris: Guillaumin et Cie, 1848), p. 527.

[23] Ibid., p. 527.   [24] Ibid., p. 505.

[25] Malthus, *Principles of Political Economy*, 2nd edn., pp. 1, 432, 434; T. R. Malthus, *Definitions in Political Economy* (London: John Murray, 1827), p. 2.

[26] Jean-Baptiste Say, *A Treatise on Political Economy*, trans. Clement C. Biddle (Philadelphia: Grigg & Elliot, 1834), pp. xxviii–xxix; [Samuel Bailey], *Observations on Certain Verbal Disputes in Political Economy* (London: R. Hunter, 1821), pp. 37, 62; Jones, *Literary Remains*, p. 598; Nassau W. Senior, *Four Introductory Lectures on Political Economy* (London: Longman, Brown, Green, and Longmans, 1852), pp. 23, 33; John Stuart Mill, *Essays on Some Unsettled Questions of Political Economy* (London: John W. Parker, 1844), pp. 129–132.

[27] Say, *A Treatise on Political Economy*, p. xxvi.

apparent consideration that mathematics might be used to contribute to *conceptual clarity* rather than to derive numerical predictions. Cournot pointed out that mathematical analysis was used "not simply to calculate numbers" but to find "relations."[28] But, like the rest of his pathbreaking work, this made no impact whatever on classical economics. Ricardo, however, saw Malthus' argument as to the empirical uncertainty of economics as an excuse for analytical sloppiness: "Political Economy, he says, is not a strict science like the mathematics, and therefore he thinks he may use words in a vague way, sometimes attaching one meaning to them, sometimes another and quite different. No proposition can surely be more absurd."[29]

Sometimes the idea that "scientific" economics meant a set of empirical propositions with a high degree of certainty might have been inferred from some of the more exuberant statements of the Ricardians that some conclusions in economics were "as certain as the principle of gravitation,"[30] "established beyond all question,"[31] "perfectly conclusive,"[32] and "unanswerable,"[33] that they possessed "all the certainty of a mathematical demonstra-

[28] Augustin Cournot, *Researches into the Mathematical Principles of the Theory of Wealth* (New York: Augustus M. Kelley, 1960), p. 3.
[29] Ricardo, *Works*, VIII, 331.   [30] Ibid., VI, 204.
[31] John Ramsey McCulloch, *A Treatise on the Circumstances Which Determine the Rate of Wages and the Condition of the Labouring Classes*, 2nd edn. (London: G. Routledge & Co., 1854), p. 8.
[32] James Mill, *Elements of Political Economy*, 3rd edn. (London: Henry G. Bohn, 1844), p. 240.
[33] John Stuart Mill, *Collected Works*, Vol. IV: *Essays on Economics and Society*, p. 16.

tion."[34] The theme of certainty was sometimes reinforced by tautologies used in defense of empirical propositions—notably Say's Law. One of the more remarkable predictions of this period was that of Robert Torrens: "With respect to Political Economy the period of controversy is passing away, and that of unanimity rapidly approaching. Twenty years hence there will scarcely exist a doubt respecting any of its fundamental principles."[35]

It is understandable how the emerging scientific emphasis of economics as a method of analysis could be mistaken for a belief that its empirical results would approach the degree of certainty found in the natural sciences. Both critics and defenders of the Ricardian tradition confused the two ideas from time to time. However, the Ricardians, in their more sober moments, clearly understood the difference between (1) systematically developing general principles, subject to exceptions and modifying circumstances, and (2) making concrete predictions from a priori assumptions. Ricardo wrote to Malthus: "Our differences may in some respects, I think, be ascribed to your considering my book as more practical than I intended it to be. My object was to elucidate

---

[34] Ibid.

[35] Robert Torrens, *An Essay on the Production of Wealth* (London: Longman, Hurst, Rees, Orme, and Brown, 1821), p. xii; twenty-one years later, Nassau Senior noted how "far" economics was from firmly establishing its doctrines, principles, or definitions. Nassau Senior, *Four Introductory Lectures on Political Economy*, p. 53. Still another twenty years after this, John E. Cairnes was to make very similar observations contrasting the state of economics with Torrens' prediction. John E. Cairnes, *The Character and Logical Method of Political Economy* (New York: Augustus M. Kelley, 1970), p. 20.

principles and to do this I imagined strong cases that I might shew the operation of those principles."[36]

Later he wrote of Malthus: ". . . it is one of my complaints against him that he does not answer your principles but wishes to shew that you have taken your case so wide, that it could under no circumstances exist; but however limited might be your case, the same principle is involved, and it is that which should be answered."[37]

Whatever the difficulties of proceeding by general principles or "theory," Ricardo saw this as unavoidable, even by so-called practical men who imagined themselves to be sticking to "facts" and "experience." He charged that such men who are "all for facts and nothing for theory . . . can hardly ever sift their facts," and remain "credulous" unconscious theorists.[38] John Stuart Mill likewise saw that "those who disavow theories cannot make one step without theorizing."[39] The only real question was whether theorizing should be done explicitly and systematically or implicitly and with no check. Whately also argued that the avowed empirical or "practical" man was "likely to form, unconsciously, an erroneous theory."[40] He said:

Man is so formed as to theorize unconsciously; facts *will* arrange themselves in his mind under certain classes, without his having any such design; and thus the materials he has been heaping together, will have

[36] Ricardo, *Works*, VIII, 184; see also ibid., III, 205.

[37] Ibid., VIII, 235.

[38] Ibid., III, 181; see also pp. 173, 239.

[39] J. S. Mill, *Essays on Some Unsettled Questions of Political Economy*, p. 142.

[40] Richard Whately, *Introductory Lectures on Political Economy*, 2nd edn. (London: B. Fellowes, 1832), p. 230.

been, as it were, building themselves up, into some, probably faulty system, while he was not aware of the process going on in his own mind.[41]

One could not "trust to accumulation of facts as a *substitute* for accuracy in the logical processes."[42] Few of the critics of classical economics—in its contemporary Ricardian form—had claimed that facts could replace theory. Many had invoked Adam Smith as an example of a *combination* of theoretical principles and empirical research.[43] Certainly Smith's systematic testing of the subsistence wage hypothesis[44] contrasts both with Ricardo's definitional approach to the subject[45] and with Malthus' aimless factual discussions used to *illustrate*—but not to test—the Malthusian population theory.[46] Sismondi was perhaps representative of contemporary critics of the Ricardian approach when he said:

It is a natural habit of the human mind to seek to reduce all its operations to the simplest formula, to

[41] Ibid., p. 235.   [42] Ibid., p. 237.

[43] [T. R. Malthus], "Political Economy," *Quarterly Review*, January 1824, p. 334; Sismondi, *Nouveaux Principes*, I, 63, 69; Say, *A Treatise on Political Economy*, pp. xl–xli.

[44] Smith, *Wealth of Nations*, pp. 74–75.

[45] "The natural price of labour is that price which is necessary to enable the labourers, one with another, to subsist and to perpetuate their race, without either increased or diminution." Ricardo, *Works*, I, 193; "Notwithstanding the tendency of wages to conform to their natural rate, their market rate may, in improving society, for an indefinite period be constantly above it." Ibid., pp. 94–95.

[46] "The principal object of the present essay is to examine the effects of one great cause." T. R. Malthus, *An Essay on Population* (London: J. M. Dent & Sons, 1960), I, 5.

generalize all its rules, and to do everything that it can by one uniform procedure to avoid more complicated procedures. That habit which tends to simplify everything, to classify everything, to generalize everything, is no doubt the most essential cause of the progress of various sciences. It is not necessary, however, to abandon oneself to it in an unreflecting manner.[47]

It was not simply that Ricardo and the Ricardians constructed abstract models,[48] but that they applied the conclusions from the highly restrictive models directly to the complexities of the real world. J. B. Say considered it "a well founded objection to Mr. Ricardo, that he sometimes reasoned upon abstract principles to which he gives too great a generality."[49]

Richard Jones's criticism that the Ricardians had derived "general principles" which "have no generality"[50] went to the heart of the issue of what was meant by, and expected of, general or abstract reasoning. Certainly empirical universality was *not* expected.[51] What was sought were analytical principles, common to a wide range of similar cases—even if such principles were not decisive

[47] Sismondi, *Nouveaux Principes*, II, 115.
[48] Sismondi's writings contained many mathematical models and Robinson Crusoe examples.
[49] Say, *A Treatise on Political Economy*, p. xlix. J. A. Schumpeter was later to christen this tendency among economists the Ricardian Vice. J. A. Schumpeter, *Essays of J. A. Schumpeter* (Cambridge, Mass.: Addison-Wesley Press, 1951), pp. 150, 154; J. A. Schumpeter, *History of Economic Analysis*, pp. 472–473.
[50] Richard Jones, *Literary Remains*, p. 569.
[51] Exceptions, modifications or "disturbing causes" were readily admitted, though sometimes the analysis then proceeded as if these admissions had not been made.

in any particular case.[52] The institutional complement necessary for the practical application of abstract principles was often neglected by the early Ricardians. However, the generality of the Ricardian *principles* was not thereby impaired. Diminishing returns, Ricardian rent, and related principles of resource allocation apply in economies vastly different, institutionally, from the England of Ricardo's time. Moreover, Ricardo's systematic, deductive method of analysis applies still more widely in time and space. Therefore, despite the institutional omissions or parochialism of Ricardian economics, which gave substance to the charge that it attempted "to construct a permanent fabric out of transitory materials,"[53] John Stuart Mill could say, "Though many of its conclusions are only locally true, its method of investigation is applicable universally."[54]

The issue of analytical generality versus empirical generality was part of an even more basic issue—whether economic principles should be founded on abstract assumptions or factual premises. Those who rejected the abstract deductive approach often pointed to the complexities of the real world as a reason for preferring empiricism. John Stuart Mill saw this as a false dichotomy. Both the "theorists" and the empirical or "practical" men used systematic reasoning, starting from given assumptions, and both derived those assumptions from something in the real world. The only meaningful ques-

[52] At least, this was the classical position by the time of John Stuart Mill: ". . . it often happens that circumstances almost peculiar to the particular case or era have a far greater share in governing that one case." J. S. Mill, *Essays on Some Unsettled Questions of Political Economy*, p. 155.

[53] J. S. Mill, *Collected Works*, IV, 225.

[54] Ibid., p. 226.

tion, then, was the particular manner in which the initial premises were derived from reality:

. . . although both classes of inquirers do nothing but theorize, and both of them consult no other guide than experience, there is this difference between them, and a most important difference it is: that those who are called practical men require *specific* experience, and argue wholly *upward* from particular facts to a general conclusion; while those who are called theorists aim at embracing a wider field of experience, and, having argued upward from particular facts to a general principle including a much wider range than that of the question under discussion, then argued downward from that general principle to a variety of specific conclusions.[55]

The simple dichotomy between inductive and deductive reasoning was therefore invalid. The real difference was between direct induction from particular cases to a general conclusion—risking the *post hoc ergo propter hoc* fallacy—and a threefold process of (1) induction from wider and more general experience, (2) deduction of conclusions applicable to a specific case, and (3) empirical verification of these conclusions "without which all the results . . . have little other value than that of conjecture."[56]

Precisely because of the multiplicity of causes and the inability to perform controlled experiments—features usually cited by critics of the abstract deductive ap-

[55] J. S. Mill, *Essays on Some Unsettled Questions of Political Economy*, p. 142.

[56] John Stuart Mill, *A System of Logic* (London: Longmans, Green and Co., 1959), Bk. III, Chap. XI, Sec. 3, p. 303.

proach—Mill saw little hope of finding the cause of any
social phenomenon by direct induction from the facts of
the particular case.[57] Only a wider survey of similar elements in a variety of circumstances was likely to suggest
good working hypotheses, from which the process of
deduction and verification could proceed. But finding
the common element in a wide range of specific cases—
i.e., abstraction—was the basis of science. The complexity
of the world and the deviation of most concrete phenomena from their abstract principles was precisely what
made systematic analytical procedure—science—neces
sary. As Karl Marx expressed it in Hegelian terms: "All
science would be superfluous, if the appearance, the
form, and the nature of things were wholly identical."[58]

> . . . the vulgar economist thinks he has made a great
> discovery when, as against the disclosures of the inner
> connection, he proudly claims that in appearance
> things look different. In fact, he is boasting that he
> holds fast to the appearance and takes it for the last
> word. Why, then, any science at all?[59]

Like Mill, Marx argued that the direct reasoning from
"the real and concrete aspects of conditions as they are"
is a method which "proves to be wrong."[60] Nothing can
be done directly with "a chaotic conception of the
whole," though one can proceed from reality to "gradually arrive at simpler ideas" until ultimately "we get at

[57] Ibid., Bk. iii, Chap. x.

[58] Karl Marx and Friedrich Engels, *Selected Correspondence*
(New York: International Publishers, 1942), p. 247.

[59] Loc. cit.

[60] Karl Marx, *Critique of Political Economy* (Chicago: Charles
H. Kerr & Co., 1904), p. 292.

the simplest conception" and then "start on our return journey" to deduce conclusions, "not as a chaotic notion of an integral whole, but as a rich aggregate of conceptions and relations."[61]

Marx was one of the few economists who rejected the claim that Ricardo was "too abstract" and claimed that "the opposite accusation would be justified"—that he did not consistently restrict himself to the abstractions appropriate to the level of analysis at which he was working—a charge which Marx made also against Adam Smith.[62] No small part of the difficulties in the interpretive literature on Marxian economics derives from his use of successive approximations in *Capital*—beginning with the abstract "essence" in Volume I, introducing complications of capital turnover in Volume II, and finally in Volume III approaching "step by step" the empirical manifestations or "forms of appearance" seen by the ordinary observer,[63] and which "serve as the starting point in the vulgar conception" of economics.[64]

Given that there were to be abstractions and deductions, how should the abstract assumptions be formulated? Mill argued that it would be "mere trifling" if the assumptions bore no relation to reality. The assumption should differ from reality "only as a part differs from the whole."[65] To the degree that "the actual facts recede

[61] Ibid., pp. 292–293.
[62] Karl Marx, *Theories of Surplus Value*, trans. G. A. Bonner and Emile Burns (New York: International Publishers, 1952), pp. 231, 202.
[63] Karl Marx, *Capital* (Chicago: Charles H. Kerr & Co., 1909), III, 38.
[64] Marx and Engels, *Selected Correspondence*, p. 245.
[65] J. S. Mill, *Essays on Some Unsettled Questions of Political Economy*, p. 149.

126

from the hypothesis" there must be "a corresponding deviation" of the results from those predicted.[66] Mill apparently did not recognize that this proposition was itself an empirically verifiable hypothesis, rather than an axiomatic truth. A "slightly" unreal assumption might prove to be fatal in some cases, while a "very" unreal assumption might prove to be quite serviceable in others.

CAUSATION

Methods of analysis depend upon some assumptions—implicit or explicit—about causation, and some preconception as to what kinds of phenomena should be explained. Causation can be thought of as sequential (A causes B causes C), as simultaneous mutual determination (as in Walrasian general equilibrium), or as a confluence of "tendencies" whose net result may bear little resemblance to any of the individual elements. What one wishes to explain may also vary, from how an existing situation came about, to what elements best explain *changes* in situations, and the degree of explanation expected may range from general guiding principles to specific predictions.

During the classical period, both orthodox and dissenting economists tended to conceive of causation in a sequential sense—as distinguished from simultaneous equilibrium—though only Sismondi formalized this in period analysis,[67] and though the Ricardians were usually content to view the process "before" and "after" in comparative static terms. Ricardo's "invariable measure of value" would have determined where a change in ex-

---

[66] Ibid., p. 145.

[67] J.C.L. Simonde [de Sismondi], *De la Richesse Commerciale* (Geneva: J. J. Paschoud, 1803), I, 100–104, 104n–108n.

change-ratios had *originated*.[68] Malthus could deny a
causal role to money in cases where it was acknowledged
to be an integral part of the phenomena under discussion, if it could be shown that monetary changes were
not the "original cause" or the "mainspring" of changes
in real variables,[69] that "the variation had originated in
the supply of commodities and not in the supply of the
currency."[70]

The Marxian "dialectical" approach emphasized reciprocal interaction—a sort of halfway house between
sequential causation and simultaneous determination.
Engels referred to the "universal action and reaction in
which causes and effects are eternally changing places,
so that what is effect here and now will be cause there
and then and vice versa."[71] Cause and effect was, from
the Marxian point of view, "a hollow abstraction" in-
dulged in by those who lack "dialectics" or an understanding of "interaction," and who reason as if "Hegel
never existed."[72] In the Marxian theory of history, for
example, there was no one-way causation originating in
economic conditions, but rather a mutual interaction of
economic and other forces, with the former being considered more powerful than the latter—explaining

[68] Ricardo, *Works*, I, 17; J. S. Mill, *Principles*, Ashley edn.,
pp. 566–568; Toronto edn., pp. 578–581.
[69] [T. R. Malthus], "Depreciation of Paper Money," *Edinburgh Review*, February 1811, p. 343.
[70] Malthus in David Ricardo, *Works*, VI, 41.
[71] Friedrich Engels, "Socialism: Utopian and Scientific," Karl
Marx and Friedrich Engels, *Basic Writings on Politics and Philosophy*, ed. Lewis S. Feuer (Garden City: Doubleday & Co.,
1959), p. 85.
[72] *Letter from Engels to Conrad Schmidt*, October 27, 1890,
ibid., p. 407.

changes—whatever its importance or unimportance in explaining *states of being*.[73]

The distinction between explaining changes and explaining states of being is crucial for understanding the methodology of classical economics, though it was a distinction not made explicit by the classical economists themselves (including, here, Marx). Given multiple causation, the variable that best explains why an existing situation, relationship, or magnitude is what it is need not be the same element that best explains changes in the same situation, relationship, or magnitude. Ricardian rent theory might explain very little of existing disparities in rental payments and yet explain very much about the rise and fall of these payments over time. In terms of the Marxian theory of history, economics might explain very little of why families exist—instead of there being a wholly atomistic society or one in which people clustered in ways unrelated to biological kinship—and yet explain very much of why families have changed in the way they have from one century to another.

Ricardo's arguments about the effect of labor input on value are in reality arguments about the *changes* in labor input on *changes* in value. Such modifying circumstances as the capital-labor ratio and the occupational wage structure might be important in explaining why values are what they are; however, they were swept aside by

[73] Ibid., p. 406; ". . . in all ideological domains tradition forms a great conservative force. But the transformations which this material undergoes spring from class relations, that is to say, out of the economic relations of the people who execute these transformations. And here that is sufficient." Friedrich Engels, "Ludwig Feuerbach and the End of Classical German Philosophy," ibid., pp. 240–241. Examples cited include law (pp. 235–237) and religion (pp. 237–238).

Ricardo on grounds that for "variations"[74] in value the occupational wage structure means little, on his assumption that "it continues nearly the same from one generation to another"[75] and while "the degree of durability of fixed capital"[76] has some effect on "variations" in prices,[77] "this cause of variation of commodities is comparatively slight in its effect."[78] He was estimating "the cause of the variations in the value of commodities"[79]—a phrase occurring 200 times in the first chapter of his *Principles*, according to one scholar's count.[80] During the classical period itself, Ricardo's great critic, Samuel Bailey, repeatedly noted that what Ricardo was really doing, especially in discussions of an "invariable measure of value" was to explain *changes* in values[81] in terms of changes in labor input. This was in keeping with the general classical concern for secular growth under conditions of historically diminishing returns, in which labor input per unit of food must rise.

Similarly, Marx's *Capital* attempts to trace *changes* in the relative shares of output going to capitalists and workers over time,[82] and the social and economic implications of such changes—the "law of motion" of

[74] Ricardo, *Works*, I, 21.   [75] Ibid., p. 22.
[76] Ibid., p. 30.   [77] Ibid.
[78] Ibid., p. 36.   [79] Ibid.
[80] John M. Cassels, "A Re-Interpretation of Ricardo on Value," *Essays in Economic Thought: Aristotle to Marshall*, ed. J. J. Spengler and W. R. Allen (Chicago: Rand McNally & Co., 1960), p. 433.
[81] [Samuel Bailey], *A Critical Dissertation on the Nature, Measures, and Causes of Value* (London: R. Hunter, 1825), pp. 12, 100, 121, 122, 127n, 178n, 236, 248.
[82] Thomas Sowell, "Marx's 'Increasing Misery' Doctrine," *American Economic Review*, March 1960, pp. 111–120.

capitalism[83]—not its static price determination. After completing his analytical system in the third volume of *Capital*, Marx could say that it was only in a "vague and meaningless" sense that it could still be said that "value of commodities is determined by the labor contained in them."[84] This was *not* a change of mind between volumes, as sometimes suggested. Marx had worked out the "transformation" of values into prices in a letter written five years before publication of the first volume of *Capital*.[85] He had denied that they were identical in the first volume itself,[86] and had treated their coincidence as a rare occurrence 20 years earlier[87]—as he was to do again in the final volume of *Capital*.[88]

Much of the "institutionalist" criticism of classical economics argued that theory must explain "things as they are"—a recurring phrase in Malthus and Richard Jones as well as later in Veblen and modern institutionalists.[89] Modern theorists have argued that the practical use of

[83] Marx, *Capital*, I, 14.   [84] Ibid., III, 203.

[85] Marx and Engels, *Selected Correspondence*, pp. 129–133.

[86] ". . . average prices do not directly coincide with the values of commodities, as Adam Smith, Ricardo, and others believe." Marx, *Capital*, I, 185n.

[87] Karl Marx, "Wage Labour and Capital," Marx and Engels, *Selected Works* (Moscow: Foreign Languages Publishing Co., 1955), I, 87; Karl Marx, *Writings of the Young Marx*, ed. L. D. Easton and Kurt H. Guddat (Garden City: Doubleday & Co., 1967), pp. 265–266.

[88] Marx, *Capital*, III, 223.

[89] This phrase or a close paraphrase appears in T. R. Malthus, *Principles of Political Economy*, 2nd edn., pp. 8, 11; Ricardo, *Works*, VII, 122; ibid., VIII, 260; [Malthus] "Political Economy," p. 297; Jones, *Literary Remains*, pp. 575, 598, 600; Thorstein Veblen, *The Place of Science in Modern Civilization* (New York: Augustus M. Kelley, 1961), p. 267.

theory is to explain *changes*[90]—not states of being—and that its validity or lack of validity must be judged by how well it does that. In this, they are at one with the Marxian theory of history.[91] John Stuart Mill failed to distinguish explanations of states of being from explanations of changes.[92] The existing state of being can be thought of as the integral of all that has gone before and the changes as the derivative at the present moment, with "human nature" a large but constant factor in the equation.

One of the more elusive concepts used in classical treatments of causation was that of "tendency." John Stuart Mill perhaps best expressed what they meant when he characterized a tendency as "a power acting with a certain intensity" in a certain "direction."[93] There are no "exceptions" to a scientifically established tendency;[94] there are only *other* tendencies operating in other directions, leading to an observable course of events which is the resultant of them all.[95] But while "tendency" sometimes had this meaning, it was sometimes also an empirical generalization about the observable course of events.

[90] Fritz Machlup, "Marginal Analysis and Empirical Research," *American Economic Review*, September 1946, p. 527; Milton Friedman, *Essays in Positive Economics* (Chicago: University of Chicago Press, 1962), pp. 4, 39.

[91] Thomas Sowell, "The 'Evolutionary' Economics of Thorstein Veblen," *Oxford Economic Papers*, July 1967, pp. 193n–194n.

[92] J. S. Mill, *A System of Logic*, Bk. vi, Chap. ix, Sec. 6, p. 594.

[93] J. S. Mill, *Essays on Some Unsettled Questions of Political Economy*, p. 160.

[94] Ibid., pp. 160–164; J. S. Mill, *A System of Logic*, p. 293.

[95] J. S. Mill, *A System of Logic*, p. 292; J. S. Mill, *Essays on Some Unsettled Questions of Political Economy*, p. 162.

Whately pointed out the "undetected ambiguity" of this word which had plagued classical economics:

By a "tendency" towards a certain result is sometimes meant, "the existence of a cause which, if *operating unimpeded*, would produce that result." In this sense it may be said, with truth, that the earth or any other body moving round a centre, has a tendency to fly off at a tangent; i.e., the centrifugal force operates in that direction, though it is controlled by the centripetal; or, again, that a man has a *greater* tendency to fall prostrate than to stand erect; i.e., the attraction of gravitation and the position of the centre of gravity, are such that the least breath of air would overset him, but for the voluntary exertion of muscular force; and, again, that population has a *tendency* to increase beyond subsistence; i.e., there are in man propensities which, if unrestrained, lead to that result.

But sometimes, again, "a tendency towards a certain result" is understood to mean "the existence of such a state of things that that result may be *expected to take place*." . . . But in this latter sense, the earth has a greater tendency to remain in its orbit than to fly off from it; man has a greater tendency to stand erect than to fall prostrate; and (as may be proved by comparing a more barbarous with a more civilized period in the history of any country) in the progress of society, subsistence has a tendency to increase at a greater rate than population.[96]

The tragicomic ambiguity in the concept of tendency was brought out in an exchange of letters between Nas-

[96] Whately, *Introductory Lectures on Political Economy*, pp. 249–250.

sau Senior and T. R. Malthus on the Malthusian population theory. With elaborate politeness and indirection, Senior maintained that he and Malthus were "agreed" on "the facts of the case" and that their differences were "almost entirely verbal."[97] Senior confessed himself guilty of "error" in initially understanding Malthus to mean that a growing population pressing on the means of subsistence was "a more probable event" than the opposite,[98] but that would be "inconsistent" with facts which Malthus himself had stated, showing rising standards of living over time.[99] Malthus' replies did nothing to separate the two meanings of the word "tendency." Even John Stuart Mill, who had produced the most searching discussion of this word, and of classical methodology generally, lapsed back into ambiguity when defending the Malthusian population theory in his *Principles*, claiming that critics' corrections of "mere language" did not affect the substance of the problem, which was that population was in "too" large a ratio to the means of subsistence[100]—a meaningless statement, empirically and analytically.

Two of Marx's main arguments involved tendencies. Indeed, the whole dialectical approach emphasized internal conflicts which forced the entity that produced them to undergo a basic transformation. Analogies with metamorphoses in nature abound in Marx and Engels.[101]

[97] Nassau William Senior, *Two Lectures on Population* (London: Saunders and Otley, 1829).

[98] Ibid., p. 56.   [99] Ibid., p. 57.

[100] J. S. Mill, *Principles*, Ashley edn., p. 359; Toronto edn., p. 353.

[101] Karl Marx, *Wage Labour and Capital* (Moscow: Foreign Languages Publishing House, 1947), p. 22; Karl Marx, *Theories of Surplus Value*, p. 186; F. Engels, *Engels on Capital*, ed. Leonard E. Mins (New York: International Publishers, 1937), p. 60;

The increasing misery of the proletariat was seen as a tendency, in both the analytical and the historical sense, for the workers' share of gross output to decline. However, scholars who interpret this to mean an absolute reduction in real income have cited passages in which tendency is clearly used only in the analytical sense and followed by a statement of *counter*tendencies toward rising wages.[102] The Marxian tendency of the falling rate of profit is clearly an analytical tendency, for it is followed immediately by a whole chapter on countertendencies.[103] Marx's point here is apparently to show pressures producing class conflict—spilling over into the political sphere—rather than to be concerned with the economic resultant as such.

Ricardo and the Ricardians often reasoned as if the long-run tendencies in the Ricardian system—subsistence wages, minimal profits, stationary capital and population—were in fact generally existing conditions. Malthus fought a running battle with Ricardo on this, protesting that actual events showed these tendencies "counterbalanced by other causes,"[104] "suspended . . . for a hundred years together,"[105] and generally constituting empirical exceptions in "unusual" conditions.[106] William

---

Marx and Engels, *Selected Correspondence*, p. 485; F. Engels, *Herr Eugen Duhring's Revolution in Science* (New York: International Publishers, 1939), p. 117.

[102] Marx, *Wage Labour and Capital*, Sec. XIV, p. 67; Marx, *Capital*, I, 657-658.

[103] Marx, *Capital*, III, Chap. XV.

[104] Ricardo, *Works*, VI, 154.

[105] [Malthus], "Political Economy," p. 315.

[106] Ricardo, *Works*, VII, 215; see also Malthus, *Principles of Political Economy*, 2nd edn., p. 402; Malthus, *Definitions in Political Economy*, p. 26.

Whewell likewise deprecated the Ricardian tendencies as guides to existing conditions, arguing how strange it would be,

> . . . if a mathematical speculator concerning the physical world should teach, as an important proposition, that all things *tend* to assume a form determined by the force of gravity; that thus the hills tend to become plains, the waterfalls to eat away their beds and disappear, the rivers to form lakes in the valleys, the glaciers to pour down in cataracts. To which the reply would be, that these tendencies are counteracted by opposite tendencies of the same order, and thus have only a small share in shaping the earth's surface. The cohesion of rocks, the tenacity of ice, the original structure of mountains, are facts as real as the action of gravity; and the doctrine that the earth's surface *tends* to a level, is of small value and limited use in physical geography.[107]

Again, the objection to the Ricardian methodology was tied to the uses made of the results, and depended also on whether the Ricardian system was conceived to explain states of being or the dynamics of change. The arbitrary designation of one element as a tendency and other elements as "disturbing causes" would have had little substantial significance if the Ricardians had not slipped into the habit of regarding the former as more common than the latter. Whewell's analogy with topography would have been meaningless if the Ricardians had been explicit that they were explaining *changes* rather than the state of being—why mountains and waterfalls erode, rather than why they exist.

[107] William Whewell, "Prefatory Notice," Richard Jones, *Literary Remains*, p. xvi.

Implicit in the classical use of tendencies, counter-tendencies and resultants is the notion that causation in the social sciences follows the pattern of physics rather than of chemistry. John Stuart Mill alone made this assumption explicit. Social science was to be constructed "after the model . . . of the more complex physical sciences."[108] In physics, the effects of "joint forces" is "the same when they act simultaneously, as if they had acted one after another."[109] A parallelogram of forces shows that a body would end up at the same point whether propelled first by one force and then the other, or whether it followed a resultant produced by the simultaneous action of the same two forces. In chemistry, by contrast, there is a mutually transforming interaction, whose result is not merely the sum of its elements. Water has "different properties" from its constituents, hydrogen and oxygen,[110] sugar a taste which "is not the sum of the taste of its component elements,"[111] etc. This is why physics is a deductive science while chemistry is experimental. "Human beings in society have no properties but those which are derived from, and may be resolved into, the laws of the nature of individual man."[112] The peculiarities of group behavior—from committees to lynch mobs—were ignored.

Given the assumption that social causation follows the model of physics rather than of chemistry, it becomes possible to analyze by successive approximation. The simplest assumption may be used as a starting point and successive complications added as needed, one step at a time, reaching an end result which will be the same as if

[108] J. S. Mill, A System of Logic, p. 584.
[109] Ibid., p. 579.   [110] Ibid., p. 573.
[111] Ibid., p. 243.   [112] Ibid., p. 573.

their complex simultaneous action had been analyzed in a "realistic" model of unmanageable complexity.[113] One may "put all these effects together, and, from what they are separately . . . collect what would be the effect of all these causes acting at once."[114]

Because the nature of individual man is the analyst's starting point, Mill considered that he might derive much insight from *mental experiments* within himself.[115] Senior pointed out that these mental experiments were unlikely to accurately reflect how other men from different backgrounds would behave.[116] According to Senior, "this accounts for the constant mismanagement of the lower orders and of children, madmen, and savages, by their intellectual and moral superiors."[117] Richard Jones rejected mental experiments for very similar reasons.[118]

Although the Ricardians were often accused of "geometrical" reasoning because of their syllogisms, John Stuart Mill explicitly rejected geometry as a model for reasoning in the social sciences. This was because (1) geometry was considered inconsistent with sequential causation, being "a science of co-existent facts, altogether independent of the laws of successive phenomena,"[119] and (2) "geometry affords no room for what so constantly occurs in mechanics and its applications, the case of conflicting forces; of causes which counteract or modify one

---

[113] J. S. Mill, *Essays on Some Unsettled Questions of Political Economy*, pp. 138–140.

[114] Ibid., p. 159.   [115] Ibid., p. 149.

[116] Senior, *Four Introductory Lectures on Political Economy*, p. 27.

[117] Ibid., p. 28.

[118] Jones, *Distribution of Wealth*, p. xv.

[119] J. S. Mill, *A System of Logic*, p. 579.

138

another."[120] One geometrical principle does not affect another; the properties of a circle are wholly unaffected by whether there is a square inscribed within it or a variety of tangents touching it or numerous other circles overlapping it. Mechanics was deductive like geometry, but permitted consideration of sequences and mutual modifications of forces or tendencies.

DEFINITIONS

Although Malthus' *Definitions in Political Economy* (1827) was the only work devoted exclusively to that topic during the classical period, a number of his contemporaries dealt with the same subject. Whately even declared "a clear definition of technical terms" to be "the most important" as well as "the most difficult" point in economics. He found "ambiguity of language" or a "fault of reasoning" to be "a more common source of error" than lack of facts or misstatements of facts.[121] Samuel Bailey declared that "the strongest powers of reasoning are an insufficient security against gross error" unless accompanied by an "incessant analysis of terms and propositions" and an "intense consciousness of intellectual operations."[122] The "chameleon-like properties of language,"[123] "inaccuracy and inattention in the use of words,"[124] the ready resort to a "learned slang"[125]—general verbal care-

[120] Loc. cit.
[121] Whately, *Introductory Lectures on Political Economy*, p. 246.
[122] [Bailey], *A Critical Dissertation on the Nature, Measures, and Causes of Value*, p. xix.
[123] Ibid., p. vi.
[124] [Bailey], *Observations on Certain Verbal Disputes in Political Economy*, p. 1.
[125] Ibid., p. 4.

lessness—caused "more than half the difficulties in political economy."[126] While Malthus thought the problem centered on the use of the same term in different senses by different writers,[127] Bailey thought it was due to the use of the same term in different senses by the *same* writer at different times.[128]

Precisely because words are intrinsically unimportant, they require a great deal of attention to prevent their affecting substantive propositions about real things. People "are fond of supposing that they are engaged in a difficult investigation into the nature of things when they are only disagreeing about the meaning of words."[129] Bailey's *Observations on Certain Verbal Disputes in Political Economy* (1821) said on its last page: "The foregoing Tract will, perhaps, be rejected with contempt, as a mere discussion about words. It is so; it professes to be so. It has for its object to *prevent* some discussions about words, which *do not* profess to be so, but pass themselves off for discussions about *things*, instead of what they really are."[130] While those who appreciated the need for clear definitions and careful attention to words put very great stress on the point, there were others who not only did not attach such importance to verbal precision, but who positively opposed strict definitions, on principle. The foremost of these was Richard Jones: "I have been re-

---

[126] Ibid., p. 71.

[127] Malthus, *Definitions in Political Economy*, p. vii.

[128] [Bailey], *A Critical Dissertation on the Nature, Measures, and Causes of Value*, pp. xxii-xxiii; [Samuel Bailey], *Letter to a Political Economist*, pp. 52, 54.

[129] [Bailey], *Observations on Certain Verbal Disputes in Political Economy*, p. 16.

[130] Ibid., p. 84.

proached with giving no regular definition of rent. The omission was not accidental. To begin, or indeed to end, an enquiry into the nature of any subject, a circumstance existing before us, by a definition, is to show how little we knew how to set about our task—how little of the inductive spirit is within us."[131]

Sismondi likewise deliberately refused to give precise definitions in his later writings.[132] In his earlier *Richesse Commerciale* (1803) he not only defined his terms mathematically[133] but also defined some of the same terms verbally in a glossary[134]—a special care for definitions which was highly unusual among economists at that time. His complete reversal in his later writings was almost certainly a reaction against the Ricardians with whom he had bitterly contended over Say's Law. James Mill, Robert Torrens, and John Stuart Mill had simply defined terms in such a way as to make Say's Law an *ex post* identity.[135] Say himself had done something similar,[136] so

[131] Jones, *Literary Remains*, p. 598.

[132] J.C.L. Simonde de Sismondi, *Etudes sur l'économie politique*, II, 143; see also ibid., pp. 227, 228; I, 115.

[133] J.C.L. Simonde [de Sismondi], *Richesse Commerciale*, I, 105n.

[134] Ibid., pp. 342–348.

[135] According to James Mill, "annual purchases and sales" will "always balance" (*Commerce Defended*, p. 82). To Torrens, supply and demand were "convertible" terms (*Edinburgh Review*, October 1819, p. 470). John Stuart Mill stated that the equality of supply and demand "is not a deduction of probability," but rather "possesses all the certainty of a mathematical demonstration," because it depends on "the very meaning of the words, demand and supply" (*Westminster Review*, July 1824, p. 41).

[136] Say's very definition of "production" included sale at cost-covering prices. (*Cours complet d'économie politique*, I, 345–346;

141

much so that Bailey had declared: "These affected *ways of talking* constitute, in great part, what M. Say calls his *doctrine*."[137]

While there was general dissatisfaction among economists of the classical period with each other's use of terms, and complaints of shifting or tautological definitions, there was no general agreement on what should be done about it. Malthus preferred that when common, everyday terms were used in economics, they be used in their common, everyday sense.[138] Whately, however, argued that it was precisely "terms to which we are familiarly accustomed"[139] which produced the greatest confusion and error. This was because (1) the need for definition was not seen, due to familiarity,[140] even though the word has *several* different meanings, and (2) even if the term is specifically defined for use in a particular discipline, there will be a constant danger of "sliding insensibly into ambiguity" by using the word in one of its common popular senses.[141]

Despite Bailey's great concern for verbal precision, he opposed the widespread use of technical terms. If a tech-

---

II, 209; *Traité d'economie politique*, 5th edn., p. 195.) Leaving aside those things which were "made inconsiderably" without really "producing" anything, Say concluded that "my doctrine on markets becomes complete." *Œuvres diverses de J.-B. Say*, p. 513).

[137] [Samuel Bailey], *An Inquiry into those Principles respecting the Nature of Demand and the Necessity of Consumption Lately Advocated by Mr. Malthus* (London: R. Hunter, 1821), p. 110.

[138] Malthus, *Definitions in Political Economy*, pp. 4–5.

[139] Whately, *Introductory Lectures on Political Economy*, p. 241.

[140] Ibid., pp. 241–243.   [141] Ibid., p. 244.

nical term was borrowed from popular usage, the old connotations would continue to surround it and invite confusion.[142] New terms were also not the answer. The "*only* use of them" is where expressing the same idea without them would involve such a long string of words that the analytical connection was likely to be lost in the process.[143] Bailey did not think that this was usually the case. The initial brevity of technical terms was regarded as a short-run advantage, followed by needless, lengthy controversies due to misunderstandings. He suggested that in place of a technical term, the definition of that term could be substituted, "putting down four or five plain words here and there, instead of one that is not plain."[144] He said: "We have time enough to attend to the additional words. We have not time enough to attend to the disputes and puzzles which arise from this zeal for 'shortness.' "[145] Bailey considered much of the technical vocabulary of economics to be a result of vain imitation of more prestigious disciplines:

> To set out with a number of terms and formal defini-
> tions, gives, it is thought, an air of resemblance to
> mathematical accuracy. But the accuracy of mathe-
> matics does not consist in having many technical
> terms, which require definitions, but in having no term
> that *has not*, where it *is* necessary, a clear definition,
> and that definition constantly borne in mind.[146]

[142] [Bailey], *Letter to a Political Economist*, pp. 62–63; [Samuel Bailey], *An Enquiry into the Nature of Demand*, p. 8.

[143] [Bailey], *Observations on Certain Verbal Disputes in Political Economy*, p. 5.

[144] Ibid., p. 3.   [145] Ibid., p. 70.

[146] Ibid., pp. 5–6.

Summary and Conclusions

Economics was generally conceived of in the classical period as having a scientific core—that is a systematic analytical method—and such additional features of science as internally consistent hypothetical truths (essential elements of Say's Law) and a stock of empirically tested principles (classical monetary theory). It was universally understood that most individual economic principles had not been, and could not be, subjected to controlled experiments and so lacked the degree of certainty of conclusions in the natural sciences. Sharp differences existed as to the implications of this fact. One school of thought regarded the impossibility of achieving scientific certainty as a reason for abandoning scientific conceptual precision and scientific methods of analysis, relying more on "experience" or common sense observation. Yet for the Ricardians the complexities and uncertainties of the real world were precisely the reason for *not* relying on direct "experience"[147] *as a source of explanatory hypotheses.* Wider experience, embracing the given phenomenon as a special case, could be used as a basis for the abstraction of principles and the deduction of conclusions—which could *then* be verified empirically from the facts of the particular phenomenon.[148] John Stuart Mill, who exemplified and elaborated classical methodology more explicitly and thoroughly than anyone else, was by no means opposed to empiricism at the stage of

[147] Ricardo, *Works*, vi, 295; J. S. Mill, *Essays on Some Unsettled Questions of Political Economy*, pp. 147–148.

[148] J. S. Mill, *Essays on Some Unsettled Questions of Political Economy*, pp. 152–153, 154; J. S. Mill, *A System of Logic*, p. 592.

verification. He was indeed the first economist to systematically analyze the application of statistical theory.[149]

J. S. Mill, who best articulated Ricardian methodology, also articulated its fatal weakness—as well as exemplifying that weakness in his defenses of Say's Law, Malthusian population theory, and classical value theory. He said:

> But it is, when not duly regarded against, an almost irresistible tendency of the human mind to become the slave of its own hypotheses; and when it has once habituated itself to reason, feel, and conceive, under certain arbitrary conditions, at length to mistake these conditions for laws of nature. Let us be accustomed whenever we think of certain things, to figure them to ourselves as existing in one particular way, never in any other way, and we at last learn to think, or to feel as if we thought, that way the natural and the only possible way: and we feel the same sort of incapability of adapting our associations to any change in the hypothesis, which a rustic feels in conceiving that it is the earth which moves and the sun which stands still . . . the greatest powers of reasoning, when connected with a sluggish imagination, are no safeguard against the poorest intellectual slavery—that of subjection to mere accidental habits of thought.[150]

Ricardian economics was narrow not only in terms of its institutional base—the contemporary British economy and society—but also in terms of its theoretical aims. Al-

[149] J. S. Mill, *A System of Logic*, Bk. III, Chaps. XVII, XVIII.
[150] J. S. Mill, *Collected Works*, IV, 226; see also J. S. Mill, *A System of Logic*, p. 238.

though the Ricardian system was constructed to generate abstract, general principles which were hypothetically true under specified conditions, the conditions actually specified produced tendentious results geared to contemporary controversies over the Corn Laws, Poor Laws, etc. It was this practice which Schumpeter labeled the "Ricardian Vice," though one in which "many less brilliant economists sinned and still sin fully as much as that eminent man did."[151] Schumpeter observed:

> . . . Ricardo's was not the mind that is primarily interested in either fundamentals or wide generalizations. . . . His interest was in the clear-cut result of direct, practical significance. In order to get this he cut that general system to pieces, bundled up as large parts of it as possible, and put them in cold storage—so that as many things as possible should be frozen and "given." He then piled one simplifying assumption upon another until, having really settled everything by these assumptions, he was left with only a few aggregative variables between which, given these assumptions, he set up simple one-way relations so that, in the end, the desired results emerged almost as tautologies. For example, a famous Ricardian theory is that profits "depend upon" the price of wheat. And under his implicit assumption and in the particular sense in which the terms of the proposition are to be understood, this is not only true, but undeniably, in fact trivially, so. Profits could not possibly depend upon anything else, since everything else is "given," that is, frozen. It is an excellent theory that can never be refuted and lacks nothing save sense.[152]

[151] Schumpeter, *Essays of J. A. Schumpeter*, p. 150.
[152] Schumpeter, *History of Economic Analysis*, pp. 472–473.

The Ricardians staunchly defended not only their abstract principles, but also key empirical assumptions—*historical* diminishing returns, flexible wage rates—and a particular way of viewing the economic process—comparative statics. The methodological advance of classical economics from the loose eclecticism of Adam Smith to the systematic precision of Ricardo and the Ricardians was not without cost. These costs included (1) tendentious models based on "special cases which in the author's mind and in his exposition are invested with a treacherous generality,"[153] (2) an overlooking of questions such as dynamics—requiring different methods, and (3) perhaps most serious of all, the tautological development of substantively meaningful propositions, such as Say's Law or the wages fund doctrine.

Many of the basic methodological issues of modern economics were raised and explored during the classical period, though not ultimately settled then any more than today. The critics of classical economics launched many of the same arguments heard later from historical, "institutionalist," and other root-and-branch opponents of modern economic theory. The later criticisms, however, more often included the charge that economics was socially conservative and apologetic, and that its abstract methodology was a means of avoiding or disguising the "real" issues. Sometimes this has been linked to a more general theory that analytical (including methodological) propositions are functions of social or political philosophy. "Experience" may seem to bear this out, since most of the strongest "institutionalists" critics of economics—from Hobson and Veblen through Galbraith and contemporary "radical political economists"—have

153 Schumpeter, *Essays of J. A. Schumpeter*, p. 154.

147

been significantly to the left of most orthodox defenders of traditional economic methodology. However, this is itself an example of the difference between reasoning inductively from specific experience and reasoning deductively by abstracting from a wider experience. If the wider experience encompasses the critics of classical abstract deductive reasoning, it is clear that such critics were far more *conservative* than their methodological opponents, and no one more strongly defended abstract deductive reasoning than Karl Marx. On the whole, the critics and supporters of classical methodology covered a wide range of the political spectrum, suggesting that the generalization from later experience is incorrect. Even in the modern period, many exceptions are found to that generalization, the most striking being the methodological similarity of the Marxist Oskar Lange and the "conservative" Milton Friedman.[154] Judging from wider historical experience, there is no necessary and little factual relationship between political philosophy and economic methodology.

[154] Oskar Lange, "The Scope and Method of Economics," *Review of Economic Studies*, XIII, No. 1 (1945-1946), 19-32; Milton Friedman, "The Methodology of Positive Economics," *Essays in Positive Economics*, pp. 3-43.

Library of Congress Cataloging in Publication Data

Sowell, Thomas, 1930-
Classical economics reconsidered.

Includes bibliographical references.
1. Economics—History. I. Title.
HB75.S593   330.15'3   74-2980
ISBN 0-691-04201-2